Rise and Fall
of the
American Empire

Richard J. Bishirjian

En Route Books and Media, LLC
Saint Louis, Missouri

En Route Books and Media, LLC
5705 Rhodes Avenue
St. Louis, MO 63109
Contact us at contactus@enroutebooksandmedia.com

Cover credit: Avery Easter
© 2022 **American Academy of Distance Learning**

ISBN-13: 978-1-956715-26-2
Library of Congress Control Number: 2022931002

All rights reserved. No part of this book may be reproduced, stored in a retrieval system, or transmitted in any form, or by any means, electronic, mechanical, photocopying, or otherwise, without the prior written permission of the author.

Contents

Prologue v

Introduction 1
   Birth, Growth, Senescence, and Death of an Empire 1
   Historical Timelines 5
   I—Failed Hope 6
   II—Progressive Domination 8
   III—Destabilization 10

Chapter 1: Celebrity and Culture 19

Chapter 2: How We Got Here: Founding of a Democratic Republic 31
   Declaration of Independence of 1776 32
   America Viewed as a Protector of Natural Rights 38
   The Natural Law View 38
   The Constitutional Convention of 1787 39

Chapter 3: The Real Constitution 45
   Federal vs. National 46

Chapter 4: Opposition to National Power 57
   The Antifederalists 57
   Nineteenth Century Whigs 64

Chapter 5: How We Got Here: Political Religion and Empire Millennialism 67

American Transcendentalists and Civil War 69

Chapter 6: How We Got Here: Progressives and World War I 77
Herbert Croly 77
Woodrow Wilson 79
World War I 83

Chapter 7: FDR and LBJ: The Making of a Modern State .. 87
Progressives and the Great Depression 87
The New Deal 89
The Great Society 91

Chapter 8: Growth of Empire in the Modern Age 97
The Cold War 97
Anti-Communism 101
After the Cold War 102

Chapter 9: The Rise of American Empire 115
Rise of Islam 119

Chapter 10: Why "Thousand Year Reichs" Fall 127
I. The Political Religion of the American Empire is a Nineteenth-Century Ideology 129
II. Expectation of Universal Peace is Not a Real Possibility 132
III. The Rule of Law, Political Rights, and Constitutional Government are the Antipodes of Egalitarianism, Universal Rights, and the Will to Impose Plebiscitary Democracy on Non-Western Cultures 133

IV. Underlying the Imposition of Hypostatized Concepts of Liberty, Democracy, and Peace on Other Countries is a Complex of Secular Messianism, Moral Arrogance, and Ignorance of Political Philosophy... 135
   V. The Willingness of Progressive Internationalists to Forget Justice at Home. The American Empire Pursued by Woodrow Wilson without Ignored Justice at Home 136

Appendix 1: Madison's Notes.. 139

Appendix 2: Port Huron Statement 163

Appendix 3: The Sharon Statement 183

About the Author 185

Prologue

This study of American Empire is based on a premise: the country that was new in 1789, when its constitutional order was ratified, no longer exists. The Constitution of the United States, consequently, intended to order and organize our politics, has been challenged to the breaking point.

I use the adjective "our" and not "their" because I am writing from the perspective of my participation in the American nation as a citizen. I "belong" to this country, and I understand that its Constitution is vital to the peace and stability of our civil society. When it changes, I am affected personally; thus, this study is not written by a passive observer.

The transition from a "democratic republic" to an empire was due to several factors. One such historical source of this development was the collapse in 1991 of America's nemesis, the Soviet Union. That threat held us together, but tensions and divisions in American society had been long coming, largely because of the many wars of the twentieth century.

War hastens the growth of "the State," Michael Barone concludes in his magisterial study of the role of government from the New Deal to the election of Ronald Reagan. "World War II, not the New Deal, produced big government in America—with steeply progressive taxes and increased interference in the details of people's daily lives."[1]

By the time the United States was engaged in a war in Vietnam, all of the ingredients for an American Empire were in place. As time passed from that war, all that was necessary to effect a change in the form and reach of how America was governed was for the character of American citizens to change.

When that occurred, the social and political order of an American Empire took command—beginning in the period of anti-Vietnam War protests in 1968—and the United States entered the equivalent of a "Hundred Years' War."

During the 116 years from 1337 to 1453, France and England fought for control of France in what in the nineteenth century came to be called the Hundred Years' War.[2]

A century in historical time defines what we call an "era," and the United States is well along the way in its transformation from democratic republic to empire.

If an aspiring American emperor, Donald Trump, can call impeachment proceedings "treason," then we know that we elected an American chief executive who viewed himself as having "imperial" powers, not an elected president representative of citizens of a democratic republic. That, of course, *is* treasonous, and the presidential election of 2024 may form the future course of American government for a hundred years.

If the worst case possible occurs, we will enter a period of civil war like that experienced by Spain. But we get ahead of our story. We must begin by defining what we mean by American Empire. We do not mean territorial control like that of the British Empire.

Niall Ferguson explores the rise of a British world order begun in "a maelstrom of seaborne violence and theft" expanding in migration of indentured servants and then the sale of slaves.³ Then came escape from religious restrictions in England by Protestant Puritans. That is the juncture in time when we pick up the American aspect of our story of the journey toward an American Empire. Between the founding of Massachusetts Bay colony by Jonathan Edwards (1703–1758) and the formation of a constitutional order in 1787, and today, something has subtly changed the priorities of American citizens.

Ambitious citizens among us redirected their lives. Whereas before, the ambitious among our young aspired to elective office hoping to join the ranks of America's greatest statesmen, they now quickly conclude that the rewards of elective office in an empire are insufficient to the demands. Others motivated by ideology, or simply desiring to "do good," seek employment in the opportunity-rich public sector.

From that perspective, even politicians who desired to restrain the imperial powers of empire and spoke longingly of a return to limited government were themselves symptomatic of structural changes in the political "system."

A prime example is the former actor Ronald Reagan. Despite continual references to fundamental principles of the Constitution, President Reagan's appeal and electability derived not from his advocacy of limited government but from his celebrity. And once in office, representatives of the imperial order were designated to run the American government.

Forty years after Ronald Reagan was elected in 1980, we witnessed a struggle by representatives of the Big Government Party to constrain the pretensions to imperial power by one president and replace him with a "Progressive" president.

The Big Government Party merely pretends to want to constrain the emperor while actually lusting to take his place. That transformation from a democratic republic into empire was little noticed. Yet the signs were evident by the inability of those who represented themselves as defenders of traditional order to generate effective leaders.

What makes members of the Congress of the United States and governors of American states ineffective in opposition to growth of an American Empire will be examined by reference to the origins of our constitutional order and historical events that shaped a vast and intrusive administrative state that, now, is beyond the control of elected members of the federal government.

Transition from a nation of "governors" and "governed" to one of "rulers" and "ruled" is at the heart of the American Empire.

Introduction

Birth, Growth, Senescence, and Death of an Empire

Because the death of everything living is preceded by a natural process of birth, growth, and senescence, death is an end point for all "being things." *Rise and Fall of the American Empire* examines, therefore, the growth of the United States into an American Empire and what causes will lead to its inevitable death.

The suggestion that the American democratic republic is now an American Empire contains both an observation and a judgment.

What is it about democratic regimes that leads them to self-destruction, to suicide? How does this condition come about, and what are the likely consequences?

We, the citizens of the United States, are participants in Western culture and inhabit patterns of thought, of living, of faith, of tradition, and of ritual that we inherited from a civilization that followed upon the fall of ancient Rome. From that past, we have inherited all the glories of "the West" and, presumably, have learned something from that experience.

We learned, for example, that it took about a thousand years for the city of Rome to grow a republic and transform that republic into a Roman Empire. And it took about five hundred years from the fall of Rome to the reestablishment of civilization in the West, what historians call "first Europe."

How, if we study the history of Rome or ancient Greece, can we avoid the same fate as the Romans and the Greeks?

That was a question that the Framers of the Constitution of the United States asked. Following their studies of the history of ancient Rome and the cities of ancient Greece, they designed a constitution on principles that limit the power of a government. They hoped that would assure the nation's survival as a democratic republic.

The American Founding Generation studied well and shaped the thirteen former English colonies from a community of disparate states into a nation.

The Framers of the Constitution sought a government that deterred the misuse of power and directed power to good ends. They understood also that man's fallen nature required that power must be checked and that those institutions of government granted power must be balanced by competing powers. Underlying this mechanical concept of checks and balances was a homogeneous spiritual community of Protestant Christians shaped by historical events in England that drove them to the American colonies.

That history of England included wars that forced upon a monarch a Magna Carta, wars of religion, the execution of Charles I, authoritarian rule by Oliver Cromwell, restoration of the monarchy, and the deposing of another king and his replacement in a "Glorious Revolution." All of that affirmed the placement of limits on the English monarchy and assured the growth of representative government.

Relations between England and the American colonists were irreparably injured by Britain's treatment of the American colonials during the French and Indian War, and that assured that the colonists would seek their independence from the British Crown. This led to the founding of an independent United States that is now—more than 232 years later—showing signs of transition into empire.

To be perfectly clear, we argue that American political culture is experiencing disorders that originated in the abandonment of the Western philosophic and theological traditions that once shaped what came to be called "Christendom."

In America, the Framers of the Constitution of the United States did the best they could with materials that were at hand. Those materials included concepts of law, historical experience, religious history, and philosophical concepts that met the exigencies of their times. But by 1787, the influence of the Enlightenment had transmitted not merely practical concepts of organization and powers but viruses that would threaten civil society hundreds of years later.

During and after the American Civil War, the homogeneous community of Protestant Christians in the American South and North was shaken by the brutality of war and by scientific theories that cast doubt on Christian revelation. American colleges that once cherished their responsibility to transmit their Protestant faith and knowledge of the civilization of the West became handmaidens of "the state." An American centralized, bureaucratic, administrative state, emulating the concentration of political power in France before its revolution, came into existence. It then too often subverted the consent of the governed with government-by-special-interests and the interests of governmental agencies.

American society, too, is now besieged by claims to government largess and of "rights" to engage in actions that America's religious culture rejected centuries ago and rejects still.

Islamic radicals believe that the West's culture is degenerate and have fashioned a political religion that justifies murder and terror. The United States government engages in a war against Islamic terrorism, but it justifies violation of the privacy of American citizens in the conduct of that war.

A sense that American culture has been dumbed-down is confirmed by college-educated citizens who know nothing of their history and by celebrities who never studied government, history, economics, or foreign policy, yet feel themselves qualified to seek public office.

This reading of decline of the American democratic republic in the twenty-first century, if accurate, could not have been predicted in 1787, but something like it was feared.

Educated colonists of what came to be called the Founding Generation of mid-eighteenth century America had read ancient history, law, and philosophy and knew that rule by masses of uneducated citizens who cared for pleasure absent civic responsibility was the downfall of what ancient Greeks and Romans called "democracy." Fortunately, for the ancient Greeks and Romans, periodically, but only in times of crisis, great men rose to meet the needs of their days and to restore order.

In 2016, apparently in utter despair that the American two-party system of government had not engendered the leadership these times require, American citizens voted for a television celebrity, Donald Trump, who began to define the nature of the United States as an empire. When he lost his bid for re-election, he claimed that "the election was stolen" and organized an attack on the nation's Capitol to delay certification of the election of Joe Biden.

Never in the history of the United States had a sitting president attempted to circumvent the process for election of a chief executive established by the Constitution of the United States. The future course of American politics had suddenly been saddled with the realization that the republic was experiencing a transformation into an empire.

Historical Timelines

Historical timelines can be useful in understanding, not merely justifying, that insight. They can show epochal moments when there was a beginning, an upward ascent, or a downward descent that had a beginning and an ending. The timeline traveled in this book takes us to an ending of American democracy, and an ending of the life of a nation-state whose mores, philosophical traditions, and laws have nourished and supported the freedom and traditional order of American society.

What future shape the American nation takes depends on whether we, the citizens of the United States, have the stomach to engage in a review of what the traditional order of the West is, and which of the disorders that beset it have driven American democracy to elect a president with no government experience and no articulated political philosophy—a president, even, whose private life is lacking in the virtues we seek in persons we elect to powerful government office. Our friends, the citizens of the nations of Europe, will sympathize with us, for they have seen it all.

A historical timeline of recent American history reveals the decline of American democracy that is mirrored in three moments, or historical developments, that have a bearing on the condition of political culture in Western Europe.

I—Failed Hope

The first moment began with the "Progressive movement," the election of Woodrow Wilson and America's entry in World War I. That was followed by the Great Depression during which traditional views were displaced by a desperate American people seeking relief from economic depression. Germany and Italy found a solution in totalitarianism.

In the United States during that era, concepts of limited government and classical economic liberalism were out of favor as a popular president began to build a centralized bureaucratic administrative state. A second World War was fought after which the United States faced formidable enemies in the totalitarian Soviet Union, People's Republic of China, and North Korea. After American leaders came to their senses and began to understand the nature of totalitarianism in Stalin's Russia and Mao Tse-tung's China, what was left of the opposition to communism was intellectually weak (the liberalism of John F. Kennedy and his successor Lyndon B. Johnson) or shoddy—anti-communism forever disgraced by the antics of a Republican politician, U.S. Senator Joseph McCarthy (R–WI), or the popular John Birch Society.

Slowly, and largely under the influence of European émigré scholars who fled Europe during the rise of Nazi Germany, influential works were published that became mainstays by the bedsides or in the libraries of a growing intellectual class of business leaders, journalists, educators, and politicians who had come to understand that they were neither socialists nor communists. Frederick Hayek's *Road to Serfdom* (1949), Eric Voegelin's *New Science of Politics* (1952), and Russell Kirk's *The Conservative Mind* (1953) are three books that come to mind.

Oddly enough, by the time their ideas took political form in the election of 1980—the epochal moment in an American political renaissance—the beginning of the end of a once virile conservative political movement was well underway. A renaissance of the ideas of America's Founding Generation had occurred too late. One can have power *and* ideas, but if pursuit of power pushes out ideas, then both are lost.

Unlike post-World War II England, Germany, and France where Winston Churchill, Ludwig Erhard, Konrad Adenauer, and Charles De Gaulle shaped a new political order in Western Europe, until the election of Ronald Reagan in November 1980, American national power was controlled by leaders of the old mindset. That mindset was characterized by a banal ignorance of a dominant "liberal" ideology that promised to drain American industry of entrepreneurs, tax citizens at confiscatory levels, dumb down American students in public schools, and send Americans to fight in a series of imperial wars. "Do-gooders" attained control of Protestant churches and religious colleges. During that era, only entrepreneurial business enterprises shaped a protected space where economic freedom could thrive, at least, for their owners and heirs.

The influence of political and economic conservatives was found in the realm of ideas where they excelled. By 1960, it was generally recognized that political and economic conservatives were "idea-rich," and the "do-gooders" who fashioned the "New Deal," "the Fair Deal," the "New Frontier," and "Great Society" were, after more than thirty years in power, "idea-poor."

That era of richness of fresh ideas, of venerable well-understood traditions, and the free space of entrepreneurial business enterprises awaited a new beginning that never came.

II—Progressive Domination

The second epochal moment that enables us to chart the decline of American democracy and the rise of an American Empire began when traditional scholars in the humanities and social sciences lost their meager grip on academic positions in higher education.

Though conservatives were idea rich, by 1970, conservative college graduates had a very difficult time finding graduate schools with scholars who would educate and protect them, and, besides, there were few jobs in academe for aspiring scholars. With Republican members of Congress and think tanks ginning up programs and policies for aspiring candidates for the office of president, why earn a postgraduate degree?

By the end of the 1980s, and certainly by 2000, there were, and still are, departments of economics that feature market-oriented economists—sometimes called "capitalism" departments—but very few humanities and social science departments that were rooted in the theological and political principles of the Christian culture of the West.

That is unfortunate because you can't educate future leaders of nations with bean counters alone.

Literature, history, art, philosophy, theology, music, even architecture are central elements of what Russell Kirk called "the conservative mind" and, in those fields, academe no longer countenanced the presence of tradition-minded scholars.

Young scholars today will never encounter the equivalent of Steven Tonsor, Russell Kirk, Eric Voegelin, Gerhart Niemeyer, Mario Pei, Donald Treadgold, Harry Jaffa, Leo Strauss, Walter Berns, Stanley Parry, Allan Bloom, or many other "greats" who left their mark on the American academic community. These types of thinkers are no longer welcome in academe. After they left their academic positions, those positions were not filled by persons of similar ability and tradition.

But perhaps the worst that was to occur was the capitulation of American universities to student rioters in the late 1960s and early 1970s. That "failure of nerve" by college administrators of the era revealed that our intellectual classes and the colleges and universities they administered lacked the character required of persons in authority. We can appreciate their hesitancy to act. College students had become instruments for revolution by high school teachers and college professors who were disappointed that revolution by the working class predicted by Karl Marx was not likely to occur.

They decided there was more than one way to achieve control than by confiscation of the means of production.

We may strive to secure our own personal futures, and the futures of our children and grandchildren, but their fate is largely out of our control because of events that occurred in 1968 and 1973.

A question asked here, "Is it too late to save the American democratic republic from the demands of empire?" yields uncomfortable answers.

So great has the office of president of the United States and the vastness of the imperial administrative state become that only the word "imperial" can explain its influence and its character of an empire.

III—Destabilization

The twentieth century ushered in a century of destabilization that resulted from America's intervention in World War I, and that fateful intervention determined the rise of an American Empire.

President Woodrow Wilson, a former president of Princeton University, believed that by entering the European War, begun in 1914, he could destroy balance-of-power politics and replace it with a system of international law. That was the origin of the influential internationalist faction in both Democrat and Republican Parties that has shaped American politics and government from the administrations of Woodrow Wilson through Joe Biden.

As a consequence of "the Great War," the Russian monarchy and the Hapsburg monarchy were replaced, and those who understood power (not mere legalities)—Vladimir

Lenin and Joseph Stalin in Russia, Adolph Hitler in Germany, and Benito Mussolini in Italy—took control and dominated East, Central, and Western Europe.

As a consequence, another generation of citizens of Western democracies was recruited to fight yet another—a "Second"—World War.

But it didn't end there.

Those families in Europe whose fortunes were destroyed after World War I would lose what fortunes they had regained along with their lives and freedom in a Cold War between totalitarians and Western democracies. The "fortunate" survivors suffered for seventy-five years in Soviet-dominated East and Central Europe and lost everything again.

Asians familiar with the twists and turns of fortune have learned to purchase gold jewelry and precious gems. In good times, they wear them, and, in bad times, they sew them into the hems of garments so that they might walk to more stable environments with something other than worthless currencies.

In light of this past history, democratic regimes seem unable to find the leaders that each generation requires, and the citizens of democracies suffer from the loss of influence of persons who share a traditional knowledge and understanding of the philosophic basis of Western civilization. Those people elected were too often prone to accept the intellectual corruption of the ideas first formulated in Revolutionary France.

Ideas do have consequences, however.

In Asia, the Truman administrations cut off support for the nationalist regime of Chiang Kai-shek and watched passively as Mao Tse-tung established a communist totalitarian regime in China that was sugar-coated by Western intellectuals who ignored Mao's totalitarian ideology and focused on his "agrarian reforms."

Military leaders like Generals Douglas MacArthur and George Patton raised the alarm but were swatted down, while the Soviet Union consolidated its hegemony in East and Central Europe, and Mao-Tse tung and Kim Il Sung repelled the United States in Korea.

The subject populations of nations of regions in the West and Asia lost faith in the West at the same time that intellectuals in the West were persuaded by ideas counter to the Western Tradition of philosophy and Christian theology.

Faith in the theological and philosophic principles of the West was mocked by our intellectual classes in 1945 and, especially, today, when belief in any tradition denominates the faithful as a privileged caste.

But, in Asia, the loss of China, and America's quick acceptance of pursuit of American interests in Korea as a United Nations police action, failed to educate the American people that the United States was at war with a totalitarian ideology. In July 2018, boxes draped in the flag of the United Nations containing remains of Americans killed in Korea were returned. But, the Trump administration didn't have the wit to replace the UN flags with American flags.

President Roosevelt's reliance on Stalin and loss of China ushered in an anti-communist movement as a domestic political force in American politics and led to the election in

1952 of the first Republican president since the New Deal, Dwight Eisenhower, the former Allied commander of the forces that won World War II. The failures of Eisenhower's successors (John F. Kennedy at the Bay of Pigs and Berlin, and Lyndon Johnson and Richard Nixon in Vietnam) again revealed the weakness of America's Enlightenment ideology.

After President Nixon decided to play the China card and move the United States away from a foreign policy of anti-communism, the policy of détente, domestic price controls, and the Watergate scandal persuaded American voters to take another chance on the Democrats.

Americans elected a president whose incompetence in national security policy allowed a shift in power in Southern Asia that established a radical Islamic regime in Iran. Though the seizure of American diplomats in Tehran was a legitimate cause for immediate military action, President Jimmy Carter did not act.

Forty-two years after granting diplomatic recognition to the People's Republic of China (PRC) as the legitimate ruler of mainland China and Taiwan, the political classes in the United States still did not comprehend the damage done to American national security.

In some ways, this was surprising since Jimmy Carter was a U.S. Naval Academy graduate and, presumably, educated in military science. But he did not act prudently toward the PRC, and his inaction toward Iran permitted a radical Islamic regime to remain in power, where it still threatens the survival of Israel and seeks to dominate Pakistan, India, and the Arab states.

Diplomatic recognition of the People's Republic of China by President Carter was followed by increased trade with China, in hope that trade would bring peace and that political differences would be overcome by a vast Chinese market for American goods. Expectations that trade would change a totalitarian state into a commercial republic were illusory. In fact, the Communist Party of the People's Republic of China used income generated from trade with the West to grow the power of its military and to lay plans to dominate Taiwan and South Korea, and, most importantly, to settle old scores with Japan.

Very old Americans, or younger ones who are well-read, remember Will Rogers's remark that "when the Judgment Day comes civilization will have an alibi, 'I never took a human life, I only sold the fellow the gun to take it with.'"

As a consequence, American political influence in East and South Asia was diminished even as America's importance as provider of military weaponry increased.

In Europe, the slowing of new births is increasing the influence of non-Christian populations whose higher birth rates and immigration into European Union states from Syria, Iraq, and Afghanistan challenge the ability of European cities to maintain order. European political leaders who acted as if they consider Europe's Christian traditions as *equal* to the traditions of all other civilizations, including Islam, have aroused a resurgent nationalism.

Europe, buffeted by a bullying Russian kleptocracy and organized into a fractious "European Union," ceases to lead the West in international affairs and is becoming insignificant in terms of geopolitical power. Cities of Western Europe today, and some countries like Spain and Portugal, are becoming significant only as interesting tourist destinations.

This realignment has not escaped Russia's attention, and post-Soviet Russian leaders are slowly attempting to absorb former satellites of the Soviet Union into Russia's sphere of influence. Russia will strive to make Ukraine and the Baltic states—every nation formerly dominated by the Soviet Union—subjects of Russia's kleptocracy.

Only insofar as a rising Islam and a powerful China challenge Russia will the United States and Russia discover a mutuality of interests. Where does that leave America?

In one word—vulnerable.

We are vulnerable to Islamic terrorists, vulnerable to an electorate ill-educated for an economy that relies less on manufacturing and more on technological skills, vulnerable to wage stagnation, vulnerable to moral decline in culture, and vulnerable to all the weaknesses of democracy.

In America, the great promises of an independent democratic republic with individual liberty, freedom of enterprise, constitutional limits on government power, and the rule of law have been called into question. No viable community of belief exists to secure the survival of the blessings of American liberty in a dangerous world—and of American power in a destabilized Western Europe.

A British Labour government elected at the end of World War II destroyed that country's economy. In the United States, welfare and entitlement programs such as Social Security established by Franklin Roosevelt's New Deal; Lyndon Johnson's welfare programs in the Great Society; and the social welfare policies of Richard Nixon, George H. W. Bush, and George W. Bush drowned the American economy in financial obligations that compel the United States to adjust its foreign policies to accommodate those to whom the United States is indebted.

At the same time, the retirement futures of young working Americans are impoverished.

The observation that, after a prolonged period of drought, we should ask, "Is this a desert?" raises the question of whether deeper problems, ones turning on the nature of Western Civilization itself, are at work. They compel us to look at our present condition and engage in a philosophical re-examination of the intellectual foundations of the West.

If so, who will engage in these philosophical discussions?

College-educated citizens have lost, or never learned, philosophy as a way of discovering truth. All is relative, they are taught, and many have come to believe it.

The method employed in this book, therefore, runs counter to the normal way that we address these political problems, which is to ignore them.

We bring to bear on the questions asked here all that we know and were taught about philosophy, theology, the civilization of the West, and Western culture. That learning is informed by a career as a college teacher and university president.

In addition to teaching courses in political theory, modern ideology, American national government, and Constitutional law, this author answered the call of service in the administration of President Ronald Reagan, served on a transition team in the Office of the President-Elect, and accepted nomination to a sub-cabinet post at the United States International Communication Agency (USICA).

This author has also edited a collection of essays about "public philosophy" that informs American democracy with insight into discoverable, public truths that have guided American politics from its beginning.[4]

That public philosophy can be seen in the author's 2015 study entitled *The Conservative Rebellion*,[5] where it is argued that the United States is the beneficiary of a sustained tradition of rebellion—not revolution. The spirit of that rebellion engendered America's independence from Britain and has arisen at critical times in our history when it seemed that democracy in America was on the wrong track.

That rebellion, however, has been hampered by a "Left University" system that dominates American colleges and universities on which we rely for education and intentionally denies to generations of students the knowledge of fundamental truths that have sustained democracy in America since the first colonists arrived in the New World.

Since the late 1960s, furthermore, our secondary schools, colleges, and universities have abdicated their responsibility to educate students in their responsibilities as citizens of a self-governing democratic republic. That opened a torrent of ignorance, permitting acceptance of an American Empire as it rooted its powers in American government and the way Americans think.

1.

Celebrity and Culture

The instability that Americans are experiencing in their politics is due to features unique to democracy in America and to all democratic regimes.

First, in principle, democracies tend to deter the best and the brightest from seeking elective office and tend to elevate the less gifted to positions of political leadership. That is exacerbated by another feature, that of celebrity. Persons who are known for their "knownness" have become attractive candidates for high office.

We are living in an age in which celebrity has become a criterion for election to public office. This is not mere "name recognition" but reflective of character associated with celebrity.

How the rise of a "Celebrity Culture" came about was first examined in 1961 by Daniel Boorstin in *The Image: or What Happened to the American Dream.*

In a distinguished career, Boorstin was librarian of Congress from 1975 to 1987, professor of history at the University of Chicago, and author of a three-volume study of America: Vol. I, *The Americans: the Colonial Experience* (1964); Vol. 2, *The National Experience* (1967); and Vol. 3, *The Democratic Experience* (1974).

In some ways, *The Image: or What Happened to the American Dream* can be viewed as the first in this series of studies of America. Boorstin writes that "since about 1900, we seem to have discovered the processes by which fame is manufactured."⁶ Since the turn of the last century, an increasing proportion of our experience consists of pseudo-events.

Boorstin defines "pseudo-events" as "an ambiguous truth" (23). Examples of pseudo-events are television quiz shows, which are "elaborately contrived situations . . . purported to inform the public" (41). Our experience is directed toward performance, not content. That explains why in the 1960 presidential debate, surveys showed that John F. Kennedy won the televised debate, but those who listened on the radio thought that Richard Nixon won.

There are also substantive changes that have occurred to reshape how we experience reality. Boorstin calls them the "dissolution of forms" (133-9). In literature, the formal structure of the literary form, language, rhetoric, vocabulary, and dramatic structure are inseparable from idea. With the introduction of abridged books, all that has been excised, and only the ghost of formal reality remains (149).

"The shadow has become the substance" (133).

These substance-less shadows may be seen in the introduction of motion pictures. Movie stars were manufactured and made distinguishable from mere actors by their "well-knownness" (154). The star became what Boorstin called a pseudo-event, "a definable publicizable personality" (156).

Even universities became celebrities, known for their well-knownness (168). And works of art came to be valued by how widely they were reproduced (126).

All this changed our consciousness of our own selves: our personality became "the attention-getting image of ourselves, our image of our own behavior" (202).

Chapter 1: Celebrity and Culture

In the era of celebrity in which we live, where "the shadow has become the substance" (204), we must ask if our politicians are the source of the disorders of this era or are we, the American people who elected them, that source?

Alexis de Tocqueville in *Democracy in America* raised important questions about democracy in France and in America. Six issues that concerned Tocqueville explain the rise of celebrity culture in the United States today. These are as follows:

1) The attack on traditional order in eighteenth-century France by the French *philosophes* and Enlightenment ideas that guided our Founding Fathers when it came time to fashion a government for a new nation;
2) Mediocrity of elected officials in all democracies;
3) Growth of a centralized bureaucratic state perfected in the France of Louis XIV and which Tocqueville felt was a danger as democracy in America grew;
4) Usurpation of the powers of the American states by the national government with the complicity of the Supreme Court of the United States;
5) Weakening of public customs and manners of Americans that Tocqueville thought were the bedrock on which American laws were established; and
6) A passion for equality of condition that no laws can satisfy.

These were the grave concerns that American democracy faced even in 1831 when Tocqueville visited America. Today we may add another. Under pressure to reduce civil discourse to the lowest common denominator of "sound bites," is it possible for American democracy to sustain public order and advance the common good without serious discussions?

Indeed, what are the necessary conditions for a "healthy" democracy, and can they be cultivated?

What did the Framers of the Constitution believe was possible when, in the Preamble, they declared that they sought "to form a more perfect Union, establish Justice, insure domestic Tranquility, provide for the common defence, promote the general Welfare, and secure the Blessings of Liberty to ourselves and our Posterity"?

If, today, it is not possible to ask these questions, what has changed since that more optimistic year of 1787?

"Regimes" have what Aristotle called "constitutions" that provide the foundations of civic order. Democratic constitutions, especially, are unique because they are artificial, man-made, not naturally occurring, nor are they inherited from some ancient past. Nevertheless, democratic constitutions are not mere legal forms; they are interwoven with the character of their citizens.

Shaping that character for self-government is essential for civic order. Unfortunately, we in the American democratic republic no longer do that. The civil disturbances that roiled higher education in the United States in the late 1960s and early 1970s erased civic education from the required education of American college students. Political theorist Allan Bloom believed that was an important sign that "We," all of us, now have a very serious problem.

Finally, we must ask, why do we give value to celebrities in areas outside the area of expertise that celebrated them? If an athlete excels in sport, for example, we give value to him beyond the range of skills in sport that made him famous.

Chapter 1: Celebrity and Culture

Is the phenomenon of "celebrity" indicative of transformation of the American regime into empire? Is their presence, which we celebrate, due to a deficiency on our part that makes it difficult to discern greatness, character, and virtue in ordinary citizens? Is a loss of our own virtue the root of this transformation?

Are the technologies that now shape the modern era—high speed computers, internet browsers, broadcast and cable television, Facebook, Twitter, Instagram—reshaping America into a world fixated on "celebrity" or simply giving expression to celebrity in culture now shaped by digital communication?

Is the media the problem or the messages conveyed by media and, if it is the messages, which messages?

Kim Kardashian; the many rock, punk, and rap musicians; Hollywood actors and actresses; television anchors; televangelists; and talk radio personalities that populate celebrity culture are influential, but is their influence consistent with civic order?

In recent memory, the state of Minnesota elected as its governor a former wrestler, Jesse Ventura; and a comedian to the United States Senate, Al Franken. California has elected to the United States Senate a vaudeville dancer, George Murphy; and son of a heavy-weight boxing champion, John V. Tunney, to the U.S. Senate; twice elected a weight-lifter and movie star, Arnold Schwarzenegger, as governor; and elected a singer, Sonny Bono, to the U.S. House of Representatives. California also sent a former movie star, Ronald Reagan, to the office of president of the United States, after electing him two times as governor of California. Yes, their names were immediately recognizable when they stood for election, but "name recognition" does not convey value; "celebrity" does.

Alexis de Tocqueville observed in *Democracy in America* that in the fifty years before 1831 when he toured America, "the race of American statesmen has evidently dwindled most remarkably."[7]

From 1781 through1829, the United States enjoyed presidents of distinction:

George Washington (1789–1797)
John Adams (1797–1801)
Thomas Jefferson (1801–1809)
James Madison (1809–1817)
James Monroe (1817–1825)
John Quincy Adams (1825–1829)

And then, Tocqueville observed, came mediocrity. President Andrew Jackson had experienced deprivation and hunger as a child and imprisonment, slander, injuries in duels, and victory in battle as an adult, but little recommended him for skill in, or knowledge of, government.

Though Jackson served briefly in the U.S. House of Representatives and the U.S. Senate and was appointed to serve on the Tennessee Supreme Court, that service was incidental to his celebrity. Andrew Jackson was a "celebrity" whose election in 1828 brought down the old order and introduced a form of popular democracy that was perfected by Progressives who in 1912 introduced the Seventeenth Amendment to the Constitution of the United States. That amendment provided for direct election of members of the United States

Chapter 1: Celebrity and Culture

Senate and permanently reshaped American democratic government as we practice it today.

Jackson was followed by eight presidents about whom the best we can say is that they came *before* America's great Civil War.

Martin van Buren	(1837–1841)
William Henry Harrison	(1841)
John Tyler	(1841–1845)
James Polk	(1845–1849)
Zachary Taylor	(1849–1850)
Millard Fillmore	(1850–1853)
Franklin Pierce	(1853–1857)
James Buchanan	(1857–1861)

Is it any different today?

How many of these presidents are sufficiently worthy to confer upon them the word "great"?

Lyndon B. Johnson
Richard Nixon
Gerald Ford
Jimmy Carter
Ronald Reagan
George H. W. Bush
Bill Clinton
George W. Bush
Barack Obama
Donald Trump
Joe Biden

If statesmanship is, and has been, dwindling or absent in American politics since, as Tocqueville thought, the election of Andrew Jackson in 1828—close to 193 ago—what understanding may we bring to our study to explain this history and consequences so grave that we now must recognize that we are citizens of an empire?

Donald Trump won the election for president of the United States in November 2016, defeating former U.S. secretary of state Hillary Clinton. In retrospect, we should not have been surprised that the GOP selected Donald Trump as its champion. The Grand Old Party had shown lack of conviction and imagination since the collapse of the Soviet Union. The candidates for the GOP nomination in 2016 were weak and undistinguished.

But who is Donald Trump?

"[He was a man with many mistresses, a history of shady dealings, and cronies who X characterized as 'intriguers, adventurers, and lackeys.' The president and the cabinet he formed, X knew, would never be in harmony. 'His sympathies were bound always to be elsewhere, for our points of view were not only different but naturally contrary. We wanted to make the republic live; he wished to inherit from it. We offered him no more than ministers when he needed accomplices.'"[8]

This description could have been written by a contemporary writer about President Donald Trump in 2016, but it was not. Mr. "X" in the above citation is Alexis de Tocqueville who was describing Louis-Napoleon, Napoleon Bonaparte's nephew.

Elected to serve as president of France for one term, when in 1851 he was denied another term, Louis-Napoleon conducted a *coup d'état*. That revolution was a consequence of the French Revolution of 1789.

Unfortunately, we know all too well who President Biden is.

Anyone who watched Senate confirmation hearings in October 1987 in which Judge Robert Bork was "borked"[9] by then senator Joe Biden would know that fairness, knowledge of the Constitution, and prudence are not aspects of President Biden's character.

Judge Bork was as good a Supreme Court nominee as they come and presented an opportunity to recognize principle over partisan politics, an attitude one cannot find in Joe Biden the politician.

Biden, at age seventy-nine, reveals visible signs of mental decline yet willingly accepted being used by his party because the price was right.

In order to become president of the United States, Biden appeased radicals who would make the District of Columbia a state, convert energy production from fossil fuels to wind and electricity, add additional seats on the U.S. Supreme Court and seat far-Left jurists, admit Muslim refugees fleeing disarray in Syria and Afghanistan, tax the rich, blow up the financial integrity of the U.S. dollar by expanding the administrative state, reward politicians whose pension funds are bankrupt, and advance democracy by military intervention—i.e., war—with nations that haven't a clue about its meaning or value.

While American government was successfully shaped by the Philadelphia Convention of 1787 and ratification by the states that approved a "Bill of Rights," traditional political order in France had been shredded by the French Revolution of 1789. That pivotal event revealed the grave weaknesses of the *Ancien Régime* in France and commenced the transformation of Western democracies into outposts for revolution. In this period in history, there developed a division in every Western democracy between tradition and revolution. At the end of the twentieth century, knowledge of where we had been from the fall of Rome to the Renaissance had been lost, and our democratic republic was transformed.

Henri de Lubac, S.J., observes in *The Drama of Atheist Humanism*[10] that four ideologies infected civilization in the West with destructive effect, namely (1) the *esprit revolutionaire* of the French Revolution in the eighteenth century, (2) the German idealism of Fichte, Hegel, Schiller, and (we observe) its American variant, "transcendentalism," (3) the atheist humanism of Karl Marx, and (4) the "positivism" of August Comte in the nineteenth century. Our study of the rise of empire requires an understanding of the first three of the above infections.

It took many years to diagnose these ideologies properly, but not before the *Ancien Régime* of France was destroyed, and what came to be understood as "totalitarian" movements overtook Russia, Germany, and Italy, threw Western Europe into two world wars, and submerged the United States in military engagements in Korea and Vietnam.

Because of the depth of this disorder of the human spirit, which political theorists have identified as political "religion," it is impermeable to rational argument. Once the acolytes of these ideologies gain control of nations, they can be countered only by force of arms. Before then, only the fundamental laws, and constitutions of regimes, can save entire nations from disaster.

Today, that recovery requires that we examine where we were *before* we got to this point of decline in intellectual culture in the West.

2.

How We Got Here: The Founding of a Democratic Republic[11]

The life of the American nation and the character of American democracy have been shaped by the Constitution of the United States, which was framed by delegates to a convention in Philadelphia in 1787 and ratified by conventions in the American states in 1789.[12]

Interpreting that Constitution is an art form that has been conducted by the Supreme Court of the United States and every American with an opinion since 1803 when Mr. Justice John Marshall asserted the principle of judicial review in *Marbury v. Madison.*

We attempt to explain "how we got here"—from 1803 to 2022, a period of 219 years during which the United States grew to become a world power administered by a bureaucratic centralized "state."

The concept of state, as opposed to "political community," was first used in the vernacular by Machiavelli. And there is a Machiavellian aspect to our use of the concept state. For us, the concept state is pejorative and connotes transformation of our form of representative government into a system of governmental control of society by a new class of experts whose claims to power are based on their assumption of superior knowledge.

That growth in the power of the state follows a course traversing a series of wars from a Civil War, World Wars I and II, a Cold War, and development of a celebrity culture.

Each era, or event, except the present era, was shaped by political ideas. Our era is the exception because of the absence of any ideas of merit.

We begin our history of pivotal moments over the past 242 years with examination of the Declaration of Independence in 1776 and the Philadelphia Convention in 1787 that framed the Constitution of the United States. We then examine the Civil War, World War I, the Great Depression followed by the Cold War of the twentieth century, and the present twenty-first century, during which America has struggled to discover its defining idea.

Declaration of Independence of 1776

Before we can understand "the world," we must first understand ourselves. That understanding begins with the Declaration of Independence and the Constitution of the United States and the Enlightenment ideas contained in the Declaration. Early drafts of the Declaration of Independence were composed by Thomas Jefferson, amended slightly by a Committee on Style of the Continental Congress, and proclaimed on July 4, 1776. Jefferson wrote the Declaration to be read in its entirety, and not merely the stirring words of the second sentence:

> We hold these truths to be self-evident, that all men are created equal, that they are endowed by their Creator with certain unalienable Rights, that among these are Life, Liberty and the pursuit of Happiness.

Though Jefferson put a great deal of effort into a list of grievances that justified declaring independence of the American colonies from the British Crown, the Declaration's enduring appeal is part and parcel with what it became: a civil religion that John Dos Passos observed was a) political mutation of the Christian doctrine of the brotherhood of man; b) the fatherhood of God; and c) the belief in self-evident truths.[13]

The civil religion of the Declaration is identical to sections 1, 2, 3, 15, and 16 of the Virginia Declaration of Rights composed by George Mason and ratified on June 12, 1776.

A DECLARATION OF RIGHTS made by the representatives of the good people of Virginia, assembled in full and free Convention which rights do pertain to them and their posterity, as the basis and foundation of government.

Section 1. That all men are by nature equally free and independent and have certain inherent rights, of which, when they enter into a state of society, they cannot, by any compact, deprive or divest their posterity; namely, the enjoyment of life and liberty, with the means of acquiring and possessing property, and pursuing and obtaining happiness and safety.

Section 2. That all power is vested in, and consequently derived from, the people; that magistrates are their trustees and servants and at all times amenable to them.

Section 3. That government is, or ought to be, instituted for the common benefit, protection, and security of the people, nation, or community; of all the various modes and forms of government, that is best which is capable of producing the greatest degree of happiness and safety and is most effectually secured against the danger of maladministration. And that, when any government shall be found inadequate or contrary to these purposes, a majority of the community has an indubitable, inalienable, and indefeasible right to reform, alter, or abolish it, in such manner as shall be judged most conducive to the public weal. . . .

Section 15. That no free government, or the blessings of liberty, can be preserved to any people but by a firm adherence to justice, moderation, temperance, frugality, and virtue and by frequent recurrence to fundamental principles.

Section 16. That religion, or the duty which we owe to our Creator, and the manner of discharging it, can be directed only by reason and conviction, not by force or violence; and therefore all men are equally entitled to the free exercise of religion, according to the dictates of conscience; and that it is the mutual duty of all to practice Christian forbearance, love, and charity toward each other.

John Dos Passos, not one to neglect the value of reason, writes in his biography of Thomas Jefferson that

"[t]here was never a question in his mind that a man's freedom to exercise his reason was the highest good, or that by reason a man could reach enough understanding of the divinely invented machine of the universe to play his part as a citizen."[14]

Chapter 2: How We Got Here

Enlightenment "reason" is not the *nous* of Plato and Aristotle, however, but a form of calculation—ratiocination—that functions as a power of mind independent of transcendent or divine experience. Severed from mind understood as rooted in noetic experience of the soul as divine, or the most divine thing in us, Jefferson shaped a civil religion based on a rationalist, anti-theological, understanding of order.

Jefferson was not alone.

His understanding of the natural order as a "divinely invented machine" reflected the eighteenth-century concept of the universe as operating on principles of "laws of nature." The universe was very much like a mechanical machine. When the Federalist interpreters of the Constitution conceived of "checks and balances" as operating principles in the Constitution, therefore, they meant that the government was designed as if it were a well-balanced machine.

Jefferson was educated at the College of William and Mary where he was influenced by William Small, a physical scientist and physician. Small was criticized for the vice of "free thinking" by the college's Anglican ministers. Their influence was erased by Jefferson when he became governor of Virginia and reorganized the curriculum of William and Mary to represent the highest rational standards of the Enlightenment.

As we shall see, Jefferson's commitment to founding the University of Virginia on well-founded, scientific principles predicted the course that higher education was to take under the influence of Progressives at the turn of the twentieth century. Cut off from the religious experience of orthodox Christianity and studies in the traditions of Western civilization, "education" in the twentieth century became an instrument for the removal of experience of the sacred and its replacement with ideology and political religion.

But we get ahead of ourselves. Concepts used by George Mason in 1776 in the Virginia Declaration of Rights of "men" who "by nature" have "inherent rights" and concepts in the Declaration of Independence of "laws of nature," "unalienable rights" of men who "are created equal" have become dominant ideas in American civil society that exist alongside a Constitution intended to operate on mechanistic principles of a well-oiled machine.

In that light, some believe that the regime established by the Constitution is driven by a higher complex of more important dynamic, rational principles found in the Declaration.

In fact, there are two traditions that emerge from that fateful year of 1787.

The phrase "all Men are created equal and independent," inserted into a draft of the Declaration of Independence, reflected thinking about the equality of men in a hypothetical "state of nature." "Equality," so defined, is central to the "dead end" of the Social Contract thinkers. To these men—Hobbes, Locke, and Rousseau—the state of nature was a condition in which men live isolated and independent lives, more or less thrown upon their own resources to survive or die. Those "men" are independent, asocial, autonomous—and equal.

But the Congress struck the word "independent" from the draft of the Declaration, which suggests the alternative belief that men are social beings, dependent, and helpless

Chapter 2: How We Got Here

without the support of others in families, villages, and the greater political community.

The final draft of the Declaration states that "all men are created equal." From that we can infer that they saw man as having value, by virtue of some compact by which they left a state of nature.

But, the citizens of these early states, what we call the Founding Generation, were Protestant Christians who understood that a more significant value of man was derived from the insight in the Book of Genesis that man is made in the image of God. In other words, all men stand equally before God and thus have value in an equal obligation to treat every other man with justice.

That concept of moral right as the obligation to act justly with respect to others does not ignore differences in ability, inheritance, or character. Men are quite unequal in that respect.

Jefferson's draft and the engrossed copy of the Declaration of Independence do not speak of moral right, though, but of "unalienable rights."

Here we see the difference between the Enlightenment concept of "rights" as "things" which men possess and the Committee on Style's refinement that "all men are created equal, that they are endowed by their Creator with certain unalienable Rights."

Suddenly, the picture brightens by attributing man's unalienable rights to the act of a Creator in the Judaeo-Christian tradition.

All the same, we sense the tension in the various drafts of the document and in the minds of the generation that gave us the Constitution of the United States. That tension may be seen in two views of the American regime.

The first is a view of American politics derived from the Declaration that we can call the "Natural Rights" view and the second view hearkens back to the Western tradition we explored earlier. We call that view the "Natural Law" view of American politics.

America Viewed as a Protector of Natural Rights

All men are equal, having unalienable rights. These rights are not political rights. They are natural rights, self-evident to all men irrespective of nationality. They stand as general principles to which we as a people are committed and by which our community must be judged. Governments are founded to secure these rights. If government does not secure them for the good of civil society, that government is evil. Only the corrupt would not seek to make all Americans free and equal. When that occurs, we the people must strike down that government and exercise the right of revolution.

The Natural Law View

The institution of civil society on the American continent was an act of Providence, and we as a people must remember with gratitude our debt to the Creator who bestowed his blessings on this land.

The purpose of government is to protect life and to assure that justice prevails over injustice. The best means to achieving those ends is rule by majority and resolution of differences of opinion by peaceful means.

Our customs, manners, and traditions give us insight into the freedoms most conducive to order, justice, and the American way. We believe that all citizens should have the same freedoms. Those freedoms are uniquely American, derivative of our civic culture. They can be abrogated, but only for the common good and by our elected leaders. Those freedoms are not pre-political, existing in some asocial state because man is by nature social. They are articulated in our Constitution and the amendments to the Constitution. The democratic procedures outlined in that Constitution constitute the channel through which the life of the nation flows and the history of our national life. That history is sustained by a Providential God who is the judge of the American people and all mankind.

The Constitutional Convention of 1787

The most important documents in the history of the American political order are the Constitution of the United States and the arguments on behalf of its ratification at the Convention in Philadelphia in 1787 and in the debates of the state ratification conventions. And the most influential interpretation of the Constitution is found in the *Federalist Papers*, essays of John Jay, Alexander Hamilton, and James Madison published anonymously in New York newspapers in 1787 and 1788 under the pen name "Publius."

In that context, the Declaration of Independence is a side-show to a Constitution Jefferson affirmed was "unquestionably the wisest ever yet presented to men."[15]

What we find in the debates at the Philadelphia Convention are a deeply rooted "common sense" that sustained us at our country's beginnings and which is characteristic of the American people. That common sense is visible, even today, in social and political responses to contemporary disorders that have occurred in the history of America.

Writing from France, as the delegates to the Philadelphia Convention prepared to meet, Jefferson shared his hopes for a constitution that would affirm universal manhood suffrage, eradicate the custom of entailing property and slaves, affirm the freedom of religion and disestablishment of the Anglican Church so that no citizen would have to pay for the maintenance of a religious establishment of another man's, and eliminate slavery of immigrants to the United States.[16]

In light of the accomplishment of the Framers of the Constitution at the convention in Philadelphia in 1787, let's examine the deliberations of its delegates and learn what it teaches us about how to live ordered lives in American civil society.[17] What we discover is contrary to commonly shared opinion today that the Constitution is composed of coequal branches. The Framers fashioned a congressionally supreme government.

In 1787, as delegates to the convention in Philadelphia prepared to meet, it was generally agreed, as I earlier mentioned, that the government would follow the model of legislative supremacy. James Madison was the principal delegate behind an attempt to check the legislature by including a "Council of Revision" in the Constitution. The provision for a Council of Revision as an aspect of the new government was ultimately defeated, not once, but three times, on June 6, July 21, and August 19.

Madison was persuaded that if a revolution were to occur in America, it would be perpetrated by the Congress.

Instead, he vigorously supported the unsuccessful attempt to establish a Council of Revision as a part of the new Constitution. Thus, despite Madison's efforts, the institutional structure originally established by the Constitution left a supreme and almost unchecked legislature.

The executive was more powerful than the judiciary, but, for that reason, the Framers suspected that if any mischief were to occur, it would probably occur in the executive.

The popular myth that the Constitution established three separate but equal branches of government has, therefore, no basis in fact. The true intent of the Framers was for the Congress to be supreme because it is the nature of representative government that the most representative branch should be most powerful.

That was the view of the majority of delegates at the Philadelphia Convention and was summarized by remarks at the convention on Monday, June 4, of Gunning Bedford Jr., of Delaware, who said that absolutely no check upon the legislature should be tolerated. "The Representatives of the people were the best Judges of what was for their interest, and ought to be under no external control whatever."

How then did the false notion of coequal branches come about, and why should we be concerned? David Siemers, a University of Wisconsin political scientist, argues that this false notion first appears around 1910 in American law schools.[18]

Siemers writes, "By the late 1910s, the idea of coequal branches was 'in the language' at least among young lawyers, some of whom were undoubtedly working in politics and aspiring to high office. The idea was ripe for appropriation by those who believed that coequal branches would be beneficial."

The early 1900s were the heyday of the Progressives who successfully amended the Constitution in 1913 to provide direct election of members of the U.S. Senate. With the Great Depression and election of President Franklin Roosevelt and his "New Deal," Siemers writes, "[I]t was common to describe the branches of government as coequal." Siemers has compiled every instance of use of the term "coequal branch" in congressional speeches and hearings from pre-1850 to the 2010s and finds that use of that term reaches its apogee from the 1960s through the 2010s for a total of 1,494 times that the term appears!

Siemers traces the introduction of the concept of coequal branches to a "conservative," California Senator William Knowland, who should have known better. By Siemers's count, Knowland used the term "coequal branches" thirty-nine times.

Knowland was followed by Richard Nixon who became "the primary backer and publicist of coequality in the 1970s." Even Wisconsin conservative Congressman Melvin Laird continued the confusion!

Only one lone Republican congressman from Iowa, Steve King, disputed that the branches were coequal. Congressman King, an outlier in "the Party of Lincoln," was stripped of his committee assignments after he questioned why the terms "white nationalist" and "white supremacist" were considered offensive. A better advocate and hope in resurgence of congressional power is Sen. Mike Lee (R–UT) who in 2016 launched something called the "Article I Project."

The backers of the Article I Project want Congress to more directly control government spending, end legislative deference to agency-made regulations, and end the use of legislative cliffs in budgeting that yields forced appropriations by emergency. Their view is that "the Founders made the Congress the 'First Branch' of the federal government—the most powerful and the most accountable."[19]

A misconception about the power of the Congress of the United States fostered by Progressives has important consequences. By transferring influence to the judiciary and executive branches, the aspirations of aspiring politicians is directed away from Congress and to other pursuits.

This has had grave consequences and explains why William Shakespeare's sentiment expressed in *Henry VI*, Part 2, Act IV, Scene 2 is so compelling.

Our attorneys-at-law have made themselves into a new class that makes the judgment of voters subservient to legal procedures. Procedure is, after all, the business of attorneys, used to reorganize how we understand our constitutional order. This is an important datum in transformation of a democratic republic into empire.

This mutation of the historical record compels us to examine what actually transpired before Progressives transformed the Constitution into a vehicle for revolution.

3

The Real Constitution

The men who attended the Philadelphia Convention were elected by the state legislatures of the governments of the thirteen states and were responsible for its success—or possible failure. Unlike the delegates attending the first meeting of the Estates General in France on May 5, 1789, the Philadelphia Convention gathered experienced political leaders from the former colonies.

Six delegates had signed the Declaration of Independence, twenty-four had served in the Continental Congress, twenty-one had served in the War for Independence, ten had helped draft state constitutions, seven had served as state governors, six had signed the Articles of Confederation, and thirty-nine had served in the Confederation Congress. Three delegates had also served as administrative officers under the Articles of Confederation.[20]

Everyone who attended the convention was persuaded of the necessity to remedy the inability of the Articles of Confederation to administer the conflicting interests of the states. James Madison observed in the preface to his notes detailing the deliberations of the convention three reasons why the confederation was unable to govern:

First, the states were reluctant to relinquish their power and thwarted the efforts of the Confederation Congress. Second, the states were jealous of power in the hands of anyone else, except themselves. And third, because the Articles of Confederation gave each state an equal voice, the large states were placed at a disadvantage, which they found intolerable.

Moreover, it was generally recognized that the Articles provided no proper authority to raise funds to reduce the public debt and no authority to regulate commerce. In addition, important matters of state were conducted without the consent of Congress.

In his introductory speech of May 29, Edmund Randolph (1753–1812) pointed out further difficulties. The Articles of Confederation, he said, provided little security from foreign invasion. The national government did not have the means to check quarrels or rebellion among the states. The government could not develop adequate imposts for the regulation of foreign trade, and, lastly, because the Articles were not considered to be the supreme law of the land, they could be subverted by state statutes.

Under these circumstances, the delegates to the convention met and immediately addressed two chief areas of contention: First, was the nature of the new government to be federal or national? And, second, what was the structure of the new government? They concluded, ultimately, that the new government should be a national supremacy government with an internal principle of legislative supremacy.

Federal vs. National

Today the words "federal" and "national" government mean the same. They both describe the national government.

That was not the case in 1787.

For Americans of that time, a "federal" government was a union or confederacy of equal parties or states. For that reason, some delegates to the convention wanted to abolish the states and absorb them into a national government. That was the view of Alexander Hamilton. His was a minority sentiment; the government formed by the convention left a great deal of power to the states. But, not as much as some would have liked.

Two theoretical questions underlay the distinction between federal and national. Did the new Constitution establish a compact of states which operated together for mutual purposes and interests? Or was the new government a union of individual citizens?

James Wilson (1742–1798) of Pennsylvania observed on June 25 that "[t]he General Govt. is not an assemblage of States, but of individuals for certain political purposes—is not meant for the States, but for the individuals composing them; the individuals therefore not the States, ought to be represented in it . . . ."

Wilson's statement was made in the context of the debate concerning the nature of election of senators.

Luther Martin (1748–1826) of Maryland, and a strong states' rights supporter, contended that the national government should not govern individuals but was meant merely to preserve the state governments. The national government, he thought, should be kept within very narrow limits. For Martin, the only meaningful political relationship that Americans had was to their own states. To create a national government to govern them directly would establish a foolish, artificial relationship. He did not think that the ineffectiveness of the Confederation Congress was due to any malice on the part of the states but rather was due to their inability to meet the demands of the Congress. He also argued that to start anew with a new constitution would theoretically dissolve the state governments, throwing them back into a state of nature. In the view of Martin and his fellow states' rights supporters, any new national government—because it was the result of the compact of the states—would be limited to the powers which the states gave it.

George Read (1733–1798) of Delaware, however, conscious of the danger of the large states to small states like his own state of Delaware, wanted a national government in which the states were abolished.

Gouverneur Morris (1752–1816) of Pennsylvania indicated that a federal government was one created by a compact and based on good faith. In other words, the parties to the compact could not be compelled to act; they were only obliged. A national government, he said, was a supreme government, and was necessarily equipped with the power to coerce compliance.

James Madison (1751–1836) of Virginia thought that in a federal government the power was exercised on the states, not on the people individually. A federal government also was one that was directly responsible to the states because it was a composition of states.

Clearly, the implication of these various views of the new plan of government was contradictory. If the new government were a compact of states, then it would be a government limited to the powers divested by the states. If, on the other hand, the new government were the product of the people of the United States, then it would be limited only by the Constitution.

These ideas may sound confusing, but their importance for understanding the interest of Americans in limited government cannot be overstated. The arguments for a "federal" government in the eighteenth-century American meaning of that term were arguments to limit the scope of power of the national government. If the government created by the Constitution were exclusively "federal," then its powers would be limited to those whose powers were expressly given up—the states. All other powers were retained by the states.

We can sense the Enlightenment notion of government in this argument. The social contract thinkers argued that government was the product of consent of the governed. So, the states' rights supporters at the convention argued that the new government was the product of the states and existed only so long as it fulfilled the will of the states. If the government violated that original contract, then the contract itself would be dissolved and, as Luther Martin said, the states would be returned to the state of nature.

The issue of federal versus national government was not fully resolved at the convention. The duties facing the delegates were too much for them to ferret out every consequence of the ideas expressed on the floor of the convention. And even during the ratification debates, James Madison argued in Number 32 of the *Federalist Papers* that the new Constitution was *both* federal and national.

It was not until 1816 that an authoritative pronouncement on the issue was made by an unexpected branch of the national government, the Supreme Court of the United States. In a case dealing with "titles," *Martin v. Hunter's Lessee*, Mr. Justice Joseph Story rejected the theory of the "federal" origin of the Constitution.

The Constitution, he wrote, was established by the people of the United States, not the states themselves. The government was not carved out of existing state sovereignties, nor from the surrender of powers existing already in the states. The powers of the states are derivative of their own constitutions, and over those constitutions the people themselves were supreme.

In effect, the Supreme Court had pulled out from under the states the theoretical rug of the social contract upon which they had built their concept of a national government. Gone was the theory that the states were original parties to a contract that created the government. The term "federal" now meant "national."

Whether federal or national, what were the objects of this government, the ends for which it existed? Were they principles derived from the Declaration of Independence such as equality and unalienable rights?

Five delegates to the convention flatly stated that the object of government is the protection of property. James Madison thought that safety, liberty, and happiness were the ends of government. James Wilson took exception. Not property, he argued, but "cultivation and improvement of the human mind was the most noble object."

Search as you may, you will not find recorded in Madison's notes the idea that government exists to protect "unalienable rights." In fact, the Constitution framed at the convention did not have a Bill of Rights. What it did have was a Preamble:

> We the people of the United States, in order to form a more perfect union, establish justice, insure domestic tranquility, provide for the common defense, promote the general welfare, and secure the blessings of liberty to ourselves and our posterity, do ordain and establish this Constitution for the United States of America.

In defense of the Declaration of Independence, the Constitution did not reject the Declaration's civil religion, concerning which I earlier cited John Dos Passos's observation as "consisting of a) political mutation of the Christian doctrine of the brotherhood of man; b) the fatherhood of God, and c) belief in self-evident truths."

The Framers simply were saying that they were constructing a government, not a church, and the operations of that government are governed by a constitution.

That the plan of the convention did not include a Bill of Rights was also important. In fact, toward the end of the convention, when George Mason moved that the plan be prefaced by a Bill of Rights, the convention voted unanimously against the motion. There was insufficient sentiment in favor of a Bill of Rights.

That is not to say that the delegates did not appreciate the importance of freedom. Or that they did not at times seem to speak in ways that might be construed to mean that they thought the end of government should be the protection of unalienable rights. The thrust of the discussions at the convention, however, emphasized giving up rights in order to make a practicable government.

An individual right, to these eighteenth-century men, was a "power" to do whatever was within one's physical capability, and for that reason they thought that the conditions of political existence necessarily limited rights. For example, George Mason, who had expressed the wish that the Constitution be prefaced by a Bill of Rights, was also to move earlier in the sessions of the convention that bills of attainder be *retained* as a power of government.

A bill of attainder is an act of a legislature identifying a person or persons for punishment for a crime, often without a trial.

Three of the delegates did not sign the Constitution: Luther Martin, Edmund Randolph, and George Mason. Neither Randolph nor Mason mentioned as their reason the failure to include a Bill of Rights.

What, then, was the structure of government that Mason and Randolph thought would end in tyranny?

First, it was generally agreed that the government that would work in America was not the British model. The model they followed, as mentioned earlier, was the one practiced by the American colonies—the model of legislative supremacy.

The outline of the new government first presented on May 19, 1787, by Edmund Randolph is known as "the Virginia Plan." Randolph resolved that the new government should consist of a National Legislature, Executive, and Judiciary. The National Legislature was to consist of two branches; the lower house was to be elected by the people of the states; the upper by the lower branch. The National Executive was to be chosen by the National Legislature. Both the executive and the judiciary would constitute a Council of Revision to examine the acts of the legislature, with a veto over the acts of the legislature.

The only aspect of Randolph's plan that could be interpreted to limit the legislature was Resolution 8 that provided for a Council of Revision. The provision for a Council of Revision as an aspect of the new government was ultimately defeated. Thus, the institutional structure originally

Chapter 3: The Real Constitution

established by the Constitution left a supreme and almost unchecked legislature.

The view of the majority of delegates at the Philadelphia Convention that absolutely no check upon the legislature should be tolerated was not shared by James Madison, who observed on July 17 that it was the tendency in America for power to concentrate in the legislature because it was in the history of the states for the legislature to be supreme.

Madison's sympathies did not lie with the legislature. Madison was persuaded that if a revolution were to occur in America, it would be perpetrated by the Congress. Instead, he vigorously supported the unsuccessful attempt to establish a Council of Revision as a part of the new Constitution. The Council of Revision was to consist of the executive and members of the judiciary and was intended to revise none other than every act of the National Legislature. Thus, a veto was introduced upon all legislative enactments until, or unless, the legislature reenacted those measures.

On Monday, June 4, 1787, the debate concerning the Council of Revision began and ended with acceptance of a council without the judiciary. As stated, the proposal gave the "Executive alone without the Judiciary the revisionary control on the laws unless overruled by 2/3 of each branch."

On June 6, two days later, however, the supporters of the Council of Revision reintroduced the original motion so that the judiciary could be included in the council. That motion was defeated by a vote of 8–3.

Again, on July 21, James Wilson moved to include the judiciary in the council, but the motion failed by a vote of 4–3 with New Jersey not present, and Pennsylvania and Georgia divided. In his remarks on July 21, however, James

Wilson stated what is now known as the theory of "judicial review." This is one of the few instances where the judiciary is specifically understood to have the power of declaring a legislative act unconstitutional, and it appears obvious that the supporters of the inclusion of the judiciary in the Council of Revision had this in mind.

We should remember, however, that because this measure was defeated several times, the presumption is that the Framers did not intend to give this power to a Supreme Court. After the defeat on July 21, the supporters for a Council of Revision made another move.

On August 19, James Madison resubmitted the motion, retaining a role for what he called the "Supreme Judiciary" in the revisionary or veto process. This motion was again defeated by a vote of 8–3 with Delaware, Maryland, and Virginia voting in the affirmative.

The convention affirmed the principle of legislative supremacy and a weak judiciary. Chief among the objections to a Council of Revision was the argument that if the judiciary were to participate in the council, then their later adjudication of the law would be biased by their having participated in its formation.

One delegate approved inclusion of the judiciary in the council, John Francis Mercer (1759–1821) of Maryland, because it tended to keep them independent of the legislative power but said, nevertheless, that he "disapproved of the Doctrine that the Judges as expositors of the Constitution should have authority to declare a law void." Upon hearing this statement, John Dickinson (1732–1808) of Delaware indicated that he was strongly impressed. He thought that no power to set aside the law ought to exist.

Chapter 3: The Real Constitution

It is clear that the convention expressed varied views about the role of the judiciary, especially as to whether it should participate in the Council of Revision, or whether it had the power of judicial review. But it seems obvious that it was not the consensus that the judiciary possessed the authority to negate unconstitutional laws.

The Constitution itself says nothing about the power of judicial review and in fact makes the judiciary virtually subservient to legislative power. The Congress has the power to create the appellate jurisdiction of the court, the number of judges the court will have, the number of lesser federal courts, and their salaries and pensions.

Moreover, even those supporters of an active judiciary wanted it limited to cases of a judicial nature. The power of a Supreme Court to scan the authority of the legislature and take up questions of a political nature was rejected by the Framers because it would usurp the powers of the legislative branch.

The concept of legislative supremacy is contrary to contemporary notions of a government of separate but equal branches, and the role of the judiciary in defining what is "constitutional."

In 1787, however, popular sovereignty was associated with representative government. In *Federalist* 51, we read, "In republican government, the legislative authority necessarily predominates." The Framers believed this because they also believed the assertion in *Federalist* 46 that the "ultimate authority resides in the people alone."

That insight is the basis of representative government and is found in the election of representatives. The Framers had a profound belief that if only the people were rightly represented in a representative assembly, good government would ensue.

That view reflected recent colonial history when George III used the colonial governors and courts to carry out his policies and prohibited the meeting of the colonial assemblies. Consequently, trust in a central administration whose head was a governor or in a system of courts never developed in colonial America. They placed their confidence in representative assemblies and, under the new Constitution, the Congress. That thinking was also reinforced by the influence of Christian culture.

Christian faith held that all men were equal before God and that the judgment of their fellow man could be trusted. They held the belief that the great body of men in society had common sense and that they would exercise it in the electing of wise and virtuous representatives. Even today, Americans believe that the outcome of a process of competing interests and claims in the pursuit of the common good would be good political decisions.

The principle of popular sovereignty implies the existence of a historical community over generations of citizens now living, and those yet to be born, that participates in divine presence. Political authority residing in the people is not a power to do whatever they have in mind to do but the obligation of the people to use their authority for a common good. An elected representative is duty bound to represent not merely his constituents but also the common interests of the United States.

Not everyone was pleased.

4

Opposition to National Power
The Antifederalists

In light of the transformation of the American government from one designed in 1787 to represent the interests of the states into the centralized, bureaucratic, administrative state with imperial powers of the twenty-first century, the arguments of those who opposed ratification of the Constitution have value for understanding American politics today.

Unfortunately, the one success of the Antifederalists, amending the Constitution to add a "Bill of Rights," did not achieve its goal of limiting the national government.

In 1925, the Supreme Court in *Gitlow v. New York* stated that the First Amendment's clause, designed to protect freedom of speech from the federal government, applied also to the states through the Due Process Clause of the Fourteenth Amendment.

The Bill of Rights was intended to restrict the federal government from abridging the rights of the states. Through the judicial doctrine of "Incorporation," however, those rights have been applied as *restrictions on the states.*

The arguments of the Antifederalists against adoption of the new Constitution were based on their understanding of the nature of the new government and their fears that powers granted to the Congress were too broad, their fears of the judiciary, and, especially, the failure of the Convention to adopt a Bill of Rights.

The worst fear of the Antifederalists was that the new government would prove to become a tyranny. At the least, the Antifederalists feared the new government would become an aristocracy. In this, their fears, at least for the first 145 years were in error.

In 1932, however, the Great Depression swept Franklin Roosevelt into office and opened the way for transformation of American government into a plurality of federal agencies making up the administrative state that it has become. The fear that the new government would lead ultimately to the abolition of the states was very close to becoming reality.

The Antifederalist fear that the states would be abolished was rooted in a suspicion that certain aspects of the Constitution were secret devices by which the national government would take over certain necessary functions of the states.

Eleazar Oswald (1750–1795), printer of the Antifederalist newspaper *The Independent Gazetteer*, argued that Article 1, Sect. 4, which allowed Congress the power to set the times, places, and manner of election of Members of Congress, would enable Congress to control American government "... when the State legislatures drop out of sight, from the necessary operation of this government."[21]

Richard Henry Lee (1732–1794), in Letter II of five *Letters from the Federal Farmer*, predicted that the imbalance in power between the national government and the states would be so great that unless the powers of the states were restored, "the state governments must be annihilated, or continue to exist for no purpose."[22]

Other aspects of the plan of the convention took away powers that the Antifederalists believed were necessary for the continued existence of the states.

The Supremacy Clause (Art. 6) states that the laws of the United States shall be the supreme law of the land. This bound the states to the supremacy of national law. And the "Necessary and Proper Clause" (Art. I, Sect. 8) gives to Congress the authority to make any laws necessary. These two sections of the Constitution guaranteed what Richard Henry Lee called, in Letter I of *Letters from the Federal Farmer*, a "consolidated government."[23] That complaint proved legitimate as the national government expanded its powers.

Lee articulated the forms of government that the delegates could have chosen. There are three, he argued:

1) "Distinct republics connected under a federal head"[24];
2) A consolidated government in which all the states are done away with;
3) A government that "consolidates the states as to certain national objects" and leaves them as "distinct independent republics, as to internal police."

Luther Martin in a *Letter to the Citizens of Maryland* (March 21, 1788) asserted that the plan was "just so much federal in appearance as to give its advocates, in some measure, an opportunity of passing it as such upon the unsuspecting multitude before they had time and opportunity to examine it and yet so predominantly national as to put it in the power of its movers, whenever the machine shall be set a going, to strike out every part that has the appearance of being federal, and to render it wholly and entirely a national government."[25]

Samuel Bryan (1759–1821), writing "To the People of Pennsylvania" in Letter III of "Centinel" in *The Independent Gazetteer* (November 8, 1787), asserted that the proposed

Constitution contained a class bias "that will give full scope to the magnificent designs of the *well-born*, unchecked by *an odious bill of rights.*"[26] The stage was set, he wrote, for another Caesar who "changed Rome from the most free, to the most tyrannical government in the world."[27]

Some Antifederalists argued that the plan of the government should be amended to specifically limit the national government to strictly enumerated powers.

Delegates to the Pennsylvania ratification convention who opposed ratification complained in a joint "minority" statement that the "Preamble" that begins with the words "We the people of the United States" is not a Preamble that would preface a "confederation of the States." Thus "the powers vested by this constitution in Congress will effect a consolidation of the States under one government, which even the advocates of this constitution admit could not be done without the sacrifice of all liberty."[28]

Implied was the Antifederalist view that the Preamble should have stated, "We the States." The Antifederalist writer "Agrippa," believed to be John Winthrop (1752-1821), in Letter XVII, addressed "To The Massachusetts Convention," argued that, as written, the Preamble openly admits that the plan was an incorporation of individual citizens of the United States in which the States play no role.[29] Agrippa, in Letter XVIII, further argued that it would be easier to amend the Articles of Confederation than to abandon them and form a new constitution.[30]

Many, like the authors of *The Pennsylvania Minority*, felt that the Congress would lack the confidence of the people, that it would not be representative of their interests, and that it could not govern a nation over a large territory. Thus, the new Constitution provides for "a permanent *standing army* and a *militia* that may be objected to as strict discipline and government."[31]

This argument against the size of the territory to be governed focused on the size of the House of Representatives which, Antifederalists believed, was too small. It consisted of only sixty-five members, of which thirty-three present would constitute a quorum, of which seventeen was a majority.

Not only were the representatives too few in number, but they were also remote. That was the complaint of John Winthrop as Agrippa, in Letter XVIII.

> All human capacities are limited to a narrow space, and as no individual is capable of practicing a great variety of trades, no single legislature is capable of managing all the variety of national and state concerns. Even if a legislature was capable of it, the business of the judicial department must, from the same cause, be slovenly done.[32]

James Lincoln, a delegate to the South Carolina ratification convention, representing district ninety-six,[33] argued that the Constitution places power "into the hands of a set of men who live one thousand miles distant from you. Let the people but once trust their liberties out of their own hands, and what will be the consequence? First, a haughty, imperious aristocracy, and ultimately, a tyrannical monarchy."[34]

As so constituted, the proposed government would govern by force, not persuasion. In that context, the Antifederalists opposed the power of Congress to raise a standing army and its power to tax which, they believed, was the power to destroy. They also objected to the power of

Congress to regulate the time, place, and manner of federal elections.

Most of all, they objected to the judiciary.

Their great fear was that the Constitution created a national judiciary of such power that it would result in the destruction of the judiciaries of the states. Thus, Agrippa proposed to the citizens of Massachusetts that, among other conditions, the judicial power be severely limited.

> The judicial department shall be confined to cases in which ambassadors are concerned, to cases depending upon treaties, to offenses committed on the high seas, to the capture of prizes, and to cases in which a foreigner residing in some foreign country shall be a party, and an American state or citizen shall be the other party, provided no suit shall be brought upon a state note.[35]

And George Mason, in a letter to George Washington citing his objection to the proposed Constitution, warned of the danger presented by the judicial power:

> The judiciary of the United States is so constructed and extended, as to absorb and destroy the judiciaries of the several states; thereby rendering laws as tedious, intricate, and expensive, and justice as unattainable by a real part of the community, as in England; and enabling the rich to oppress and ruin the poor.[36]

Any idea that the judiciary could declare unconstitutional an act of Congress, or of a state, was rejected outright.

The Antifederalists demanded that a Bill of Rights that protected the states from domination by the national government must be added to the plan. That Antifederalist argument led to an agreement that the Constitution would be amended in the First Congress to include a list of rights that would never be taken from the states.

The Tenth Amendment represents that desire:

> The powers not delegated to the United States by the Constitution nor prohibited by it to the States, are reserved to the States respectively, or to the people.

Other rights to be protected were the rights of state legislatures to impose taxes; the power of the militias to remain with the states; that no treaty shall oppose existing law unless that law is repealed; that unless specifically delegated, all powers are reserved to the states; that every state shall retain its powers unless specifically delegated; and that every state shall retain the power to arm its own militia.

A close examination reveals that these rights are rights of states, not of persons. The Antifederalists did not agitate for a bill of individual rights. Yet the words they used in demanding for a Bill of Rights were confusing.

An example is this statement by Patrick Dollard a delegate at the South Carolina ratification convention representing Prince Frederick's Parish. His constituents, he said,

> are nearly all, to a man, opposed to this new Constitution because, they say, they have omitted to insert a bill of rights therein, ascertaining and fundamentally establishing, the unalienable rights of men, without a full, free,

and secure enjoyment of which there can be no liberty, and over which it is not necessary that a good government should have control.[37]

Nineteenth Century Whigs

Two policies of the first Whigs in England led by Robert Walpole (1676–1745) were low taxes and disdain of expansionist foreign policies. These English Whigs in the early eighteenth century wanted to constrain the monarchy within limits defined by common law and a history of rights established to limit it.

American Whigs, fashioned between 1833 and 1840, strode the divisions of American politics between Democratic Republicans of John Quincy Adams and Jacksonian Democrats and were committed to constraining the powers of the chief executive.

President Andrew Jackson's strenuous use of the veto and executive power shaped Whig policy. If Jackson's opponents needed proof that this president had gone too far, Jackson's call for the abolition of the Electoral College was icing on a very big opposition cake.

Two legislative giants of the day, John Calhoun and Henry Clay, struggled to constrain President Andrew Jackson's power but were defeated. Calhoun, too tied to the rights of slaveholders, ultimately was dismissed by events leading to the American Civil War and destruction of "States' Rights" as defense of the indefensible. But Calhoun sowed the seeds of secession by supporting states' rights to nullify federal law.

The tariff of 1828, enacted when Jackson was president, was designed to protect Northern industry from imports but was opposed by the Southern states led by Calhoun because of its costly effect on Southern commerce. South Carolina declared that it had the right to nullify federal law. In response, President Jackson sent U.S. Navy warships to Charleston and threatened to hang anyone supporting nullification—or secession—and asked Congress to pass a "Force Bill" authorizing military force.

Later in 1834, Calhoun, responding to an assertion by President Jackson that the president and Congress were coequal, denied the legitimacy of such an assertion. President Jackson, it will be remembered by students of Alexis de Tocqueville, was "a man of violent temper and mediocre talents." Tocqueville writes of Jackson that

> no one circumstance in the whole course of his career ever proved that he is qualified to govern a free people, and indeed the majority of the enlightened classes of the Union has always been opposed to him.

Henry Clay's influence was greater, but he too was defeated by Jackson's political genius and the difficult struggles of a young Whig Party to organize a coalition greater than the president's.

A bone of contention between the two was Clay's attempt to charter the Second Bank of the United States, which Jackson thwarted by executive veto and then by moving federal funds to state banks. That led to relaxed lending policies that, with other policies, led to the Panic of 1837 and election of a Whig, William Henry Harrison, as president.

Clay also bridled at Jackson's claim of "co-equal" standing. In response, Clay "argued most strenuously for congressional power . . . and his speeches frequently enumerate his party's belief in congressional power."[38] One speech in particular asserts the power of Congress:

> Congress should be able to override vetoes by a simple majority vote, cabinet officers should consider themselves under the direction of the law and the Constitution more than under the personal direction of the president, congressional approval should be required for the dismissal of administrative officers, the president may not change the meaning of a law through interpretation, and control of the Treasury should be in the hands of Congress.[39]

That was the anti-imperial case for constraining the imperial presidency. But there were many other voices striving to be heard that were less interested in restraining the imperial power of the American chief executive.

5

How We Got Here
Political Religion and Empire
Millennialism

Simultaneous with the philosophic approach to fashioning a new government at the Philadelphia Convention of 1787, and Whig attempts to constrain a Democrat president, there was in development a religion of democracy that was to shape the rise of an American Empire. The seeds of that development were carried to America in the millennial views of some Protestant colonists.

Jonathan Edwards (1703–1758) preached the victory over the enemies of God in this world.[40] Men of good character and millennialist beliefs who sought to establish heaven on earth have been on the American scene for generations—as may be inferred from this very long list of "preachers" cited by Ernest Lee Tuveson:

> Jonathan Edwards, Joseph Bellamy, Samuel Hopkins, Joseph Priestly, Richard Price, Timothy Dwight, Alexander Campbell, Henry Boynton Smith, Lyman Beecher, Mark Hopkins, Horace Bushnell, Enoch Pond and Josiah Strong.[41]

Their powerful religious message of redemption *in* the world breached the barrier between the City of Man and the City of God constructed in the fifth century by St. Augustine.

In the Book of Revelation, Chapter 19, John sees heaven open and a white horse ridden by one who is called Faithful and True. The armies in heaven follow him, and the nations of the earth are destroyed. The Devil is sealed in hell for a thousand years, during which time the righteous reign with Christ.

At the end of this millennium, the dead are resurrected and there occurs a Last Judgment. St. Augustine interpreted that prophecy metaphorically and rebuked those who maintained that the thousand years of the prophecy must be interpreted as meaning a worldly enjoyment of luxury on earth enduring for a thousand years.

"Fundamentalist" Christians who take a literalist approach to a prophecy of a millennium in the Book of Revelation tend to confuse biblical accounts of ancient Israel with the state of modern Israel. Many religious leaders today believe that Jerusalem should be the capital of Israel because it's in the Bible. President Donald Trump appealed to them by moving the American Embassy from Tel Aviv to Jerusalem.

What is ignored is the political reality that Israel today is not ancient Israel but a client state of the United States that would not exist were it not for the U.S. commitment to defend the state of Israel. In matters of foreign policy, the Bible should not be our guide, but our guide should be whether it is in the American interest for an international city like Jerusalem, where Muslims, Christians, and Jews have sacred ties, to become the capital of a state reviled by most of the Arab world.

Principled Christians must recognize that the United States is a nation with national interests, and the policies of

Christian politicians should be informed by that rather than by biblical prophecies. If they ignore that principle of national interest, they then open themselves to appeals to support policies that may be in conflict with the best interests of the American people.

American Transcendentalists and Civil War

A civil religion was first inspired by a stirring Declaration of Independence that spoke of truths that are "self-evident," of "laws of nature" and of "Nature's God." But, by the middle of the nineteenth century a new intellectual religion was fashioned.

German idealists who identified man with God found a response in America. German idealism replaced the Classical Greek understanding of human existence as participating in divine reality through noetic contemplation of the divine. For these idealist humanists, man *was* divine. A consequence of this combination of reasoning with spiritual desire and absolute identification of man with God was that divisions between North and South were incapable of being resolved by political compromise that could avoid a civil war.

Robert Kagan cites as evidence of this a rise of a uniquely American "moralism" that Kagan finds in the first annual address of John Quincy Adams in 1825:

> The great object of the institution of civil government is the improvement of the condition of those who are parties to the social compact, and no government, in whatever form constituted, can accomplish the lawful ends of

its institution but in proportion as it improves the condition of those over whom it is established.⁴²

American "moralism"—sense of right and wrong—was also evident in public reaction to the war between Christian Greeks and the Muslim Turks.⁴³ But, millennial chiliasts who saw divine significance in the American Revolution ratcheted up that residual morality by fashioning a millenarian ideology that forged America into a "Savior nation"⁴⁴ committed to the redemption of the world.

Without getting too deeply into the weeds of German idealism, a flirtation with the idealism of Fichte, Schelling, and Hegel was begun in England and Scotland by Thomas Carlyle and Samuel Taylor Coleridge and transmitted to America by what became known as "transcendentalism."

English philosophy was burdened by an empiricism and materialism in the seventeenth-century understanding of John Locke, and especially of Thomas Hobbes, who lived through a civil war in England and the authoritarian regime of Oliver Cromwell. The rejection of experience of transcendence in the materialism of the Social Contract thinkers led to their rejection and the appeal of sensitive spirits in nineteenth-century England to German idealists who asserted the absolute identification of man with the divine.

Johann Gottlieb Fichte conceived of history in terms of the "Divine Idea" or the life of God. Man's existence, for Fichte, is a thought of God, and the difference of kind between man and God was seen as a mere difference of degree. From this perspective, "history"—understood as the movement of divine being in development of human

Chapter 5: How We Got Here

consciousness—was moving toward a this-worldly resolution of contradictions in existence.

The American scholar Fredric Henry Hedge had traveled to Germany in 1817 to study music and was well-read in German idealism. He founded The Transcendentalist Club, which attracted Ralph Waldo Emerson (1803–1882) and Orestes Brownson (1803–1876), who attended the first meeting in 1836. Later meetings found Henry David Thoreau (1817–1862) and William Henry Channing (1810–1884) in attendance.[45]

Other prominent transcendentalists were Theodore Parker (1810–1860), William Ellery Channing (1780–1842), Margaret Fuller (1810-1850), George Ripley (1802–1880), Frederic Henry Lodge (1805–1890), Julia Ward Howe, and Howe's husband, Samuel Gridley Howe. Transcendentalist essays were published in *The Dial*, beginning in 1840, and the *North American Review*, first published in 1815.

For most Americans who express any interest, philosophy is not a search for truth, justice, or the best regime so much as a form for justifying actions that are believed to actualize truth or advance "change." Americans as a people are doers, not philosophers, and they favor men of action in a good cause.

Theodore Parker and many New England transcendentalists were enthusiastic about the Hungarian patriot Lajos Kossuth, who opposed the Habsburgs in 1848 and sought to unite east central Europe in a loose federation. Robert Kagan notes that Abraham Lincoln offered a resolution supporting the universal right of self-determination at a Kossuth meeting in 1852.[46]

Emerson's "Concord Hymn" is characteristic. Emerson expanded the meaning of the American Revolution beyond the reality of a war for independence into a Second Reality of redemption of the world by a democratic America.

> By the rude bridge that arched the flood,
> Their flag to April's breeze unfurled,
> Here once the embattled farmers stood
> And fired the shot heard round the world.

"The shot" was heard in Boston, not "round the world," but Emerson's chiliastic hopes for America were compounded by a hymn of Julia Ward Howe's, "The Battle Hymn of the Republic," published in February 1862.[47]

The hymn is a poetic, though secularized, rendition of the millennial passages of the Book of Revelation: the "glory of the coming of the Lord;" the "trampling out the vintage where the grapes of wrath are stored" (which in the manuscript version more closely approximates the scriptural language, "He is trampling out the wine press . . . ."); and the personal testimony of the chiliast who attests that she has "seen Him" in the bloody events of the American Civil War and who announces that she can "read a fiery gospel writ in burnished rows of steel."

Howe transforms Christ's redemptive mission—which is not of this world—into the world immanent social activism of the anti-slavery movement:

> With a glory in his bosom that transfigures you and me:
> As he died to make men holy, let us die to make men free.[48]

Though Howe's strident hymn may have conflicted with the meditative aspects of transcendentalism, if we search for motives that made the "movement," we read in the first issue of *The Dial* an essay entitled "The Religion of Beauty." There we find an expression of spiritual anguish: "without the open sense of beauty . . . how hard a task is faith! how hard to feel that God is here! how unlovely looks religion!"[49]

Loss of faith for persons raised in Protestant religions in the nineteenth century was common and was exacerbated by the American Civil War. The attraction of German idealism to the transcendentalists was not a solution to disorder of the spirit experienced by nineteenth-century Americans. It was a way station on the road toward framing an American political religion.

Abraham Lincoln was an example.

By utilizing biblical language in his construction of the meaning of democracy, Lincoln was a participant in a process that contributed to the acculturation of American citizens to political religion.

Some of Lincoln's religious language comes, Robert Kagan suggests, from the Second Great Awakening.[50] But much is an expression of Lincoln's genius for capturing an idea of America as a nation in a single phrase.

Richard Gamble captures Lincoln's importance. The Gettysburg Address was, Gamble writes, "an empty vessel" into which "Lincoln poured the 19th-century's potent ideologies of nationalism, democratism, and romantic idealism.

"In merely 271 words, the wartime president fused his epoch's most powerful and disruptive tendencies—nationalism, democratism, and German idealism—into a civil religion indebted to the language of Christianity but devoid of its content."[51]

Gamble calls our attention to a curious character of Lincoln's speech: "abstracted from the place where he stood and the suffering he memorialized."

Lincoln mentioned "a great battle-field" but not the town and surrounding farms of Gettysburg. He invoked the "fathers" but left them unnamed. He extolled the "proposition that all men are created equal" but left the Declaration of Independence implied.

He honored "brave men" but not a single commanding officer or soldier by name. He spoke of a "nation" five times but avoided anything as definite as geographic America, the United States, the republic, the Constitution, the North, the South, or even the Union.

Lincoln had fashioned a new secular "civil religion," an advance on Jefferson's, by stripping the historical aspects of the nation to allow for its ascension into what Gamble calls "a transcendent realm."

Lincoln fashioned a new propositional faith at Gettysburg rooted in the assertion of the Declaration that all men are created equal. Gamble refers to this as Lincoln's "propositional apriorism" and points to a passage from the 1850 sermon of transcendentalist minister Theodore Parker that Lincoln read: "Democracy is direct self-government, over all the people, for all the people, by all the people."

Lincoln's propositional nation became "less like itself and more like the emerging European nation-states of mid-century, each pursuing its God-given benevolent mission."

Kenneth Minoque observes that "even as late as the early nineteenth century, de Maistre defined the nation as 'the king and the nobility.'"⁵² In the eighteenth and into the nineteenth century, the "nation" was the ruling class. The American nation as defined by the ruling class was changed by the events of the Civil War and articulated in the influential address of Abraham Lincoln at Gettysburg in November 1863.

What for the Framers, the Antifederalists, and the Whigs, was a government of states' rights, with Lincoln the American regime became a nation committed to propositions about rights and equality.

Gamble concludes that ever since Lincoln's Gettysburg Address:

> [G]enerations of Americans have come to believe that we have always been a democratic nation animated by an Idea. The alternatives have been excluded from the national creed as heresy. The way most Americans today interpret the Declaration of Independence, the purposes of the War for Independence, the principles that underlie America's Constitution, the causes and consequences of the Civil War, and the calling of the propositional nation to the rest of the world comes largely from the Gettysburg Address.

6

How We Got Here From Progressives and World War I

In the early twentieth century, two persons, Herbert Croly and Woodrow Wilson, represented a transition in national consciousness that shaped twentieth-century American intellectual culture to the present day.

Herbert Croly

Herbert Croly's *The Promise of American Life* (1909) and later the journal *The New Republic*, which he founded and edited, performed a role in shaping the political attitudes of America's intellectual elite in the Progressive era, a role which Woodrow Wilson complemented by shaping the popular attitudes of Americans towards democracy, the nature of peace, and America's destiny.

In *The Promise of American Life*, Croly wrote: "For better or worse, democracy cannot be disentangled from an aspiration toward human perfectibility, and hence from the adoption of measures looking in the direction of realizing such an aspiration." That aspiration would be realized primarily, he thought, by those "exceptional fellow countrymen" of his, the American intellectuals whom he called "saints."

These secular saints who lead the common mass, Croly speculated, will not necessarily be conservators of the American political tradition. The realization of the promise of American life will sometimes require a "partial renunciation" of the American past and of present interests, if necessary to contribute to the "national purpose."

There may even occur a sudden transfiguration by "an outburst of enthusiasm." He observed:

> If such a moment ever arrives, it will be partly the creation of some democratic evangelist—some imitator of Jesus who will reveal to men the path whereby they may enter into spiritual possession of their individual and social achievements, and immeasurably increase them by virtue of personal regeneration.

Croly speculated that a civil religion is required that brings into view a national purpose to be realized in public affairs. This purpose requires secular saints, themselves led by a messiah who will reveal the true path.

A transfiguration will come about because the American nation itself is formed by a democratic ideal which is working its way in time towards full realization. Before this can occur, however, this democratic ideal, always a promise, must be fully articulated, its creed formulated now, so that the American people may believe once again in the promise of American life.

A critique of Croly's civil religion requires that we return to basics. Politics is a science of four principles:

1) rational judgments informed by an awareness of circumstances,
2) a proper assessment of the limits of government and abuses of state power,
3) a concern for institutions which limit power, and

4) prudent knowledge of the common good.

Croly's call for secular saints who will conduct us into a condition of reconstituted and transfigured reality has less to do with political science than with prophecy, enthusiasm, and magic.

The national life is indeed informed by an idea, by public myths which articulate the commonly shared beliefs of society's members. But that idea does not exist independently nor is it working its way in human events toward a logical fulfillment.

The national life can expire, change its form, or become something altogether different, not by means of the twists and turns of a world spirit but by the weakening or collapse of civic virtue and political judgment.

How swiftly such a collapse can occur and how vulnerable the American political system is to such collapse is visible in the influence of Woodrow Wilson's political religion.

Woodrow Wilson

Informing Woodrow Wilson's political religion is a view of history similar to Croly's. History, Wilson believed, moves according to a plan in which America plays a major role. His view of history is one of a progressive development, moving slowly but inexorably to a condition of reconstituted reality.

In an address in Pittsburgh, Pennsylvania, at a YMCA celebration on October 24, 1914, Wilson said:

> [N]o man can look at the past of the history of this world without seeing a vision of the future of the history of this world; and when you think of the accumulated moral

forces that have made one age better than another age in the progress of mankind, then you can open your eyes to the vision. You can see that age by age, though with a blind struggle in the dust of the road, though often mistaking the path and losing its way in the mire, mankind is yet—sometimes with bloody hands and battered knees—nevertheless struggling step after step up the slow stages to the day when he shall live in the full light which shines upon the uplands, where all the light that illumines mankind shines direct from the face of God."[53]

The role of America in this plan of history, Wilson was persuaded, was shaped and directed by God from the beginning. This, he declared on one occasion, is a nation God built with our hands.

To what end, we might ask?

In an address before Confederate veterans of the Civil War on June 5, 1917, Wilson declared that "we are to be an instrument in the hands of God to see that liberty is made secure for mankind."

Wilson's view of history in which America and mankind were moving toward a world-immanent transfiguration of the human condition was not an isolated facet of the thought of an otherwise pragmatic man of affairs. Instead, it was an integral aspect of his attitude towards life and the skills required if political life was to be governed rightly.

Politics, for Wilson, required "vision," and vision for Wilson meant knowledge of God's purpose in history. In his First Inaugural Address, Wilson was speaking of his own visionary politics when he described his task as "no mere task of politics."

Chapter 6: How We Got Here

Politics for Woodrow Wilson was not mere politics; politics was a special capacity to announce the immanence of a new age certified by the political leader who experienced a special revelation.

Woodrow Wilson's vision of America was one of a nation ordained to play a mighty role in history; it was only fitting, therefore, that Americans should be perceived as different from the rest of the peoples of the world. We, for example, entered World War I "for no selfish advantage." Our troops were "the armies of God." Accordingly, America undertook missions of redemption.

In St. Louis, Missouri, on September 5, 1919, Wilson observed that: "[America] has said to mankind at her birth: 'We have come to redeem the world by giving it liberty and justice.' Now we are called upon before the tribunal of mankind to redeem that immortal pledge."

Wilson was an idealist in the manner T. H. Green[54] defined as one who seeks to "enact God in the world" by the pursuit of ideals not given in experience.

Wilson was committed to the ideal of a world absent of war, a world he believed to be within the grasp of a civilized world. And America's entry into World War I was largely motivated by the desire to attain such an ideal. That it was to be accomplished by violence did not dismay Wilson.

It is important to understand that Woodrow Wilson's desire to involve us in World War I was grounded in his will to destroy the system of balance-of-power politics. Wilson's oft-repeated assertion that America had no selfish interest to be satisfied by her entry into the war, that we sought no territory, no concessions, was his way of expressing utter contempt for balance-of-power politics.

On July 10, 1919, in his address to the United States Senate presenting the treaty of peace with Germany, Wilson proclaimed:

> Every true heart in the world, and every enlightened judgment demanded that, at whatever cost of independent action, every government that took thought for its people or for justice or for ordered freedom would lend itself to a new purpose and utterly destroy the old order of international politics.

Wilson's desire to "utterly destroy" the reality of balance of powers was yoked with his desire to destroy "autocratic authority." He was persuaded that only governments governed by majority rule, not by autocratic minorities, could truly seek peace.

As a consequence, he sought to destroy autocratic governments; in the present instance, the government of Kaiser Wilhelm.

In such a "good cause," Wilson believed that the maximum use of force was acceptable. Wilson saw a "halo" around the musket over the mantle of the citizen soldier who fought to redeem the world and around the returning American troops.

Force, apparently, was not to be disdained when executed by the "armies of God."

Wilson was in search of a cause in which to destroy the existing world order and found it in "the terrible war for democracy and human rights." The war was terrible, no doubt, in part because the winners of the conflict, "the only people in the world who are going to reap the harvest of the future are the people who can entertain ideals, who can follow ideals to the death."

But the war would be terrible also because Wilson saw the war in apocalyptic terms. This war had eschatological significance. He called the war a "final contest" which would bring about a "final emancipation." And if America did not join the League of Nations, he foresaw another "final war"; for surely there would be war again, he said, one that would bring the evil policies of the powers of this world to a close.

Looking at history as a progressive movement toward a transfigured condition of peace and justice, Wilson saw himself as living in the last days when heroic acts were necessary to bring history to fruition.

World War I

Wars bring out the worst in American presidents and, like previous presidents, "Republican Senator Henry Cabot Lodge of Massachusetts... told James Bryce, the former British ambassador to the United States, that 'the President has no administrative capacity. He lives in the sunshine. He wants nobody to tell him the truth apparently and he has a perfect genius for selecting little men for important places.'"[55]

Nothing grows more quickly during war than the size, power, and intrusiveness of the state—and taxation. In World War I, Raymond Keating writes,

> [T]he top rate was pushed up to 67 percent in 1917 and 77 percent in 1918. The top rate was dropped slightly to 73 percent in 1919. The corporate income tax also was

increased, with the rate moving from 1 percent to 2 percent in 1916, 6 percent in 1917, 12 percent in 1918, and back to 10 percent in 1919. As for the economy during this period, real GNP barely grew in 1913 (0.9 percent), and then declined in 1914 and 1915 (-4.4 percent and -0.9 percent, respectively). After the war (with fighting ending at the end of 1918), the U.S. economy went into a depression, with real GNP declining by 3.6 percent in 1919, 4.4 percent in 1920, and 8.7 percent in 1921.[56]

But, as intellectual historian Mark Malvasi writes, something more sinister occurred during World War I at the behest of President Woodrow Wilson.

Victory depended on unanimity of opinion and conformity of belief. To discredit, punish, and ultimately eliminate antiwar sentiment became the first order of business. "Woe be to the man or group of men who stands in our way," Wilson enjoined Congress in June of 1917. Congress reinforced the president's warning with a series of laws enacted to quell opposition to the war effort and to silence criticism of the government.

The Alien Act, the Alien Enemies Act, the Espionage Act, the Sedition Act, and the Trading with the Enemies Act granted the federal government extraordinary power to indict, fine, or imprison anyone who disparaged or impeded the conduct of the war.[57]

Victor Berger, socialist editor of the *Milwaukee Leader*, was sentenced to prison for twenty years for violation of the Espionage Act. Eugene V. Debs[58] was sentenced to ten years

Chapter 6: How We Got Here

in prison for sedition. And most noteworthy were the Palmer Raids conducted by Attorney General A. Mitchell Palmer, during which three thousand anarchists and suspected leftists were arrested. In opposition, civil libertarians, including a future justice of the Supreme Court, Felix Frankfurter, supported creation of the American Civil Liberties Union (ACLU). When patriotism required calling sauerkraut "liberty cabbage," Americans of German descent responded by attempting to lower their profile by speaking English, changing their names, and fermenting home-made wine quietly in basement casks. German Lutherans de-emphasized church services in German.

According to Mark Malvasi, Conservative professor of English at the University of Chicago Richard M. Weaver saw Woodrow Wilson's war as having "gone a long way toward limiting the independence of mind, enabling representatives of the Wilson administration to promote and excuse conduct that decent and honorable Americans might, under ordinary conditions, have regarded as atrocities."[59] Malvasi quotes Weaver on this point:

> The advance toward totalism in this war certainly appears ... in the way in which every phase of life—economic, financial, social, and cultural—was drawn into the struggle and made ancillary to the war. To an unprecedented degree the idea was promoted that the nation should become one, with no thought but to kill and destroy. Those of mature age may recall the hysteria whipped up in this country by President Woodrow Wilson, which went even to the point of banning the playing of German music.[60]

This "totalism" was evident in the actions of Harry A. Garfield, chosen "to administer the indispensable coal and oil supply," Malvasi explains, adding that "Garfield exemplified the Progressive creed. Americans, he said, must abandon individualism once and for all time. If nothing else, individualism was inefficient and led to waste. Reorganizing the economy for war, Garfield insisted, must rest on the principles of 'cooperation' and 'combination.'"[61]

Though urged to "abandon individualism," reductions in personal and corporate taxes by the Harding and Coolidge administrations fostered individualism in the form of what came to be known as "the Roaring Twenties."

7

FDR and LBJ
The Making of a Modern State
Progressives and the Great Depression

Between the years 1870 and 1910, a modern academic enterprise took shape. Under the influence of German education exemplified by Wilhelm von Humboldt, founder of Humboldt University in Berlin, graduate education and electives were developed.

During this time, many universities abandoned their religious roots and no longer looked to ancient writers for moral lessons and political guidance. James Piereson's important study, *Shattered Consensus*,[62] attributes this to a principle of German idealism that "truth is not something known and passed on, but the product of persistent inquiry and continuous revision."

While the secular religion of idealist humanism of Kant, Fichte, Schelling, Schiller, and Hegel introduced into the United States by American transcendentalists was germinating, American college faculty were placed at the center of the academic enterprise and empowered to decide all matters dealing with curriculum, tenure, and hiring. Thus emerged what James Piereson calls "a new class of professional intellectuals."[63]

At the turn of the twentieth century, Progressives fashioned the first phase of a modem liberal ideology with a focus on making universities, and the academics who taught in them, handmaidens of government.

Leaders in this development were critics of classical liberalism who rejected the Scottish "common sense" philosophers of the Scottish Enlightenment and British empiricism.[64] Gone were David Hume, Adam Smith, Thomas Reid, Adam Ferguson, James Beattie, and Dugald Stewart.

In their place stepped, Pierson writes, Thorstein Veblen (economics), John Dewey (philosophy), Charles Beard (history), and Oliver Wendell Holmes (law). Pierson observes that "these thinkers were not only academics but more importantly graduates of the new university." All believed that the Constitution was "inadequate to the challenge of modern life."[65]

According to Gregory Brown, Progressives supported six public policies:

- anti-trust laws directed against attempts to keep prices up
- most regulatory commissions
- pure food and drug laws
- conservation
- anti-trust laws directed against business concentration
- progressive income taxes[66]

Universities whose social science faculties were Progressive focused their attention on government power used for the public interest, subjects in which they were experts.

In the late 1890s, this became visible in the "Wisconsin idea" by which universities partnered with the state to provide technical expertise to guide state legislators. Pierson writes:

> The Wisconsin idea brought out into the open a new role for the university, which was to bring experts and expert knowledge into the political process. This was one of the clearest links between the emerging university and the Progressive movement, since the university was the logical source for the experts needed to design and implement Progressive policies.[67]

During this period, the lines between teaching, on the one hand, and advocating political positions, on the other, became blurred, and campus radicals asserted that all teaching was political. With the Great Depression, Progressives took control of American universities, removed courses that explained the great tradition of classical liberalism, and vigorously supported the administration of Franklin D. Roosevelt, who put into place the makings of a modern state.

The New Deal

Michael Barone lists the actions taken in the first Hundred Days of the Roosevelt administration commencing on March 4, 1933:[68]

- ordered a national bank holiday
- passed a bill that cut veterans' benefits and federal employee pay
- urged Congress to legalize sale of low alcohol beer (prior to repeal of "Prohibition")
- introduced the Agricultural Adjustment Act

- proposed the Civilian Conservation Corps
- called for the regulation of securities markets
- called for formation of the TVA
- a Home Owner's Loan Act
- removed the United States from the gold standard and introduced the National Recovery Act
- used radio "Fireside chats" to establish a personal relationship with American voters.

The "Hundred Days," Barone writes, "created a new kind of political spectacle, one of far-reaching decisions being made by unelected and hitherto unknown administrators."[69]

In less than three months, FDR laid the foundations of the modern state. He accomplished that, Amity Shlaes writes, by avoiding the abstractions constantly opined by Republicans about free enterprise, rugged individualism, and checks and balances. Instead, FDR asked his radio listeners, "Are you better off than you were last year?"[70]

In 1935, FDR took his administration further to the left than he had dared in his first two years, "trying to put together his long-dreamed-of coalition of LaFollette Progressives, Jeffersonian Democrats, and Al Smith Catholics... and blue-collar workers."[71] FDR started by calling for an infusion of $4.8 billion for work relief, and establishment of an old age social security insurance program that exists today, a bitter-sweet legacy that burdens the youngest in the workforce by forced contributions to a program that may not exist when they qualify for retirement benefits.

By June, FDR saw passage of Social Security, the Wagner Act, a public utilities and banking bill, and a progressive tax law "including estate and gift taxes, a graduated corporate income tax, and sharply graduated taxes on high personal income."[72]

The Great Society

For conservative Americans who hoped that the death of FDR signaled the end of presidential flirtation with socialism, the next seven presidents disabused them of that hope.

Harry Truman was an enthusiastic New Dealer as were John Kennedy, Lyndon Johnson, and Jimmy Carter. Dwight Eisenhower, in many ways our first modern "celebrity" president, had few new ideas, and one would wish that Richard Nixon and Gerald Ford had none. Together, all seven, but especially Lyndon Johnson, shaped conditions that made possible the election of Ronald Reagan—thirty-five years later.

Amity Shlaes writes that in the era she calls the "Great Society," the federal government "redefined its role in the arts on television and radio, and in public schools. Washington left no area untouched."[73] That revolution was made possible by the tragic assassination of President Kennedy, the commitment to redistribution of wealth by his vice president, and the defeat of the Republican nominee, Barry Goldwater, in the election for president of 1964, which gave LBJ the White House and control of both houses of Congress.

During LBJ's presidency, a war was waged by the federal government against the rest of the nation. Relief might have been expected from the Republican, Richard Nixon, but Nixon's true intent was symbolized by his placing a portrait of Woodrow Wilson in the Cabinet Room.[74]

This tragic story of government growth capped by a land war in Asia that placed 543,000 troops in Vietnam by April 1969 sowed seeds of division in American society that have been replaced by new divisions suggesting that, as long as federal power dominates civil society, Americans will live in a "tribalized" nation.

The players in this carnival of subversion included President Lyndon Johnson, Walter Reuther, and the United Auto Workers Union; a "New Class" of influential advisors typified by Daniel Patrick Moynihan and Sargent Shriver; and socialists like Tom Hayden and Michael Harrington. Thrown into this era of change was Martin Luther King, Jr., who embodied JFK's and LBJ's civil rights reforms that, Shlaes writes, "redeemed our democracy."[75]

The spiritual face of the Great Society was inspired by Michael Harrington's writings, especially *The Other America: Poverty in the United States*,[76] and his activism, visible in shaping a meeting of young socialists in June 1962 at the UAW's retreat at Port Huron, Michigan. From that meeting sprang a manifesto known as the Port Huron Statement, which for the Left was a beacon shining light toward a socialist future. Coincidentally, and of interest to those who value constitutional order, a young William F. Buckley, Jr., assembled a group of young conservatives at his family estate in Sharon, Connecticut, where a conservative manifesto was drafted in September 1960 called the Sharon Statement.[77]

Michael Harrington was adamant that none affiliated with the Communist Party participate in drafting the Port Huron Statement and that the statement avoid criticism of American labor unions. His demands, Shlaes writes, were directed at Tom Hayden who, though like Harington was influenced by Saul Alinsky, disagreed with Harrington's distinction between socialism and communism.[78] Hayden saw no difference between North Vietnam and what he called the "corrupt" regime in the south. Later, he would visit North Vietnam in 1965. Hayden's wife, Jane Fonda, whom he married in 1973, visited North Vietnam in 1972. As a young student, Hayden founded Students for a Democratic Society and participated in founding Student Nonviolent Coordinating Committee (SNCC) at Port Huron in 1962. During the Democrat Party convention in Chicago in 1968, Hayden encouraged rioters, "saying at one point, 'let us make sure if our blood flows, it flows all over the city.'"[79]

Though Hayden was on the fringe of a radical left wing, at the center of a Great Society was Walter Reuther, a committed socialist and head of the United Automobile Workers (UAW). Reuther worked to fashion a system of benefits to abolish poverty. That, surprising some, was what motivated Lyndon Johnson.

Hated by Progressives for his opposition to civil rights reform in his role as majority leader of the U.S. Senate, within a day of the assassination of President Kennedy, LBJ reached out to Walter Reuther and directed the White House switchboard to call Reuther and ask for the phone numbers of labor leaders David Dubinsky, I. W. Abel, and Dave McDonald.[80]

LBJ wasted no time in announcing his intention to "cure poverty."[81] President Johnson was employed in the Roosevelt administration to persuade farmers in South Texas to plow over crops as a means of raising prices of farm products. He was later chosen to head the Texas office of the National Youth Administration. His commitment to aggressive management of government was symbolized by hanging a portrait of Andrew Jackson in the Oval Office. He was also an aggressive competitor who sought to eliminate or suppress those he perceived were competitors.[82]

As his administration progressed, four concerns occupied him: Vietnam, the federal budget, the ratio of gold reserves to Federal Reserve Notes, and critics in the press whom he considered to be traitors.[83] After all, LBJ achieved real reforms in civil rights, attempted to rid poverty from the lives of Americans, and created hundreds of programs that employed tens of thousands of Americans. He had emulated FDR by creating the equivalent of a Brain Trust that brought Robert McNamara, Sargent Shriver, Theodore Sorenson, and Richard Goodwin into service in his administration. All were representative of a New Class of government planners who were described by Moynihan as "scientists, social scientists who used not ideology but statistics to arrive at serious conclusions." He called this "The Professionalization of Reform."[84] Moynihan was what critics of behaviorist social science call "bean counters." Moynihan might not have bridled at that because, he said, "Progress begins on social problems when it becomes possible to measure them."[85] "Unless you are in a position to measure your results you will never be able to bring the program to a high level of efficiency much less to prove it to Congress."[86]

Like Moynihan, Sargent Shriver was representative of this New Class with the addition of ideological commitment to aggressive government action. Shriver was tapped by LBJ to head the Office of Economic Opportunity (OEO) and enlisted Michael Harrington, the guru of poverty, into the war on poverty. It would be unfair to say that Shriver liked war,

Chapter 7: FDR and LBJ

but he enlisted in the navy in WWII, serving five years, and suffered wounds in the Battle of Guadalcanal. Married to Eunice Kennedy, he served with his wife in the Justice Department building, where he managed a program to reduce juvenile delinquency.

Founding director of the Peace Corps, which position he held while serving as head of OEO, Shriver used his access to LBJ and the power of OEO to establish the Volunteers in Service to America (VISTA), a Youth Corps, Head Start, and an Office of Legal Services. His service to LBJ ended only when Bobby Kennedy announced on March 15, 1968, that he would run for president, and Johnson proposed to send him to France as ambassador. On March 31, LBJ announced that he would not run for reelection.

It was about time. LBJ needed new taxes to finance the war in Vietnam, but Rep. Wilbur Mills chose not to support a Vietnam tax surcharge. Sen. Eugene McCarthy won 41.9 percent of the New Hampshire presidential primary compared to LBJ's 49.6 percent.

More ominous for the long term were conditions created by LBJ's Great Society that led to successful entry into politics of Hollywood actor Ronald Reagan. Reagan came to prominence during the presidential campaign of Sen. Barry Goldwater when he gave a nationally televised speech titled "A Time to Choose." The 1964 election presented a choice of whether America would become collectivist or free. Reagan became a hot political prospect made even more attractive by his attack on busing students in LA schools and opposition to the California Rural Legal Assistance program. When elected in California, Reagan was the first governor not to hold a law degree, and he nominated William Clark, who never earned a law degree, to the California Supreme Court. Also, as governor Reagan cut $220 million from "Medi-Cal," California's Medicaid program and was instrumental in having Angela Davis fired from her teaching position at UCLA.

8

Growth of Empire in the Modern Age
The Cold War

The expulsion of the classical liberalism of Adam Smith and David Ricardo from higher education, accompanied by the loss of the philosophic basis of civilization in the West, left civil society without accepted principles of economics and philosophical limits on the power of government. When faced with the ideology of Marxism-Leninism embodied in a totalitarian Soviet Union, Western intellectuals lacked a means of identifying the totalitarian character of that regime.

Through the Communist Party of the USA, the Soviet Union had an uninterrupted opportunity to subvert democratic government in the United States and to infiltrate agents and agents of influence into American national government and American labor unions.

The Great Depression and the election of President Franklin Roosevelt gave intellectuals with communist ties the opportunity to serve in the new administration. Alger Hiss, John Stuart Service, Louis Howe, and many other top officials served the interests of the Soviet Union unnoticed.

The Soviet Union was an ally in World War II, and that facilitated communist infiltration. President Roosevelt presided at the 1943 conference in Tehran and the 1945 conference at Yalta in the Crimea that permitted building what later Winston Churchill called the "Iron Curtain." As a consequence of that decision, the subject populations of the regions in East and Central Europe lost faith in the West at the same time that intellectuals in the West had rejected the great philosophic tradition of Western Civilization.

Too late, Congress responded in 1938 by creating the House Un-American Activities Committee, and with U.S. interests unprotected, in 1950 Wisconsin Senator Joseph McCarthy used his position as chairman of the Government Operations Committee and its Permanent Subcommittee on investigations to bring to public attention the infiltration of communists at the U.S. Department of State.

President Franklin Roosevelt was totally ignorant of the ideology of Marxism-Leninism with grave consequences as the Allied Leaders (Roosevelt, Stalin, and Churchill) met at Tehran and Yalta to design the post-World War II world and left his successor, Harry Truman, vulnerable to charges of allowing communist infiltration.

These five statements by President Roosevelt are symptomatic of "the supposedly progressive twentieth century [that] became a saturnalia of tyranny and violence, surpassing in this respect also all previous records of such horrors."[87]

- "I have just a hunch that Stalin doesn't want anything but security for his country, and I think that if I give him everything I possibly can and ask nothing from him in return, *noblesse oblige,* he won't try to annex anything and will work for world democracy and peace."[88]
- "I think there is nothing more important than that Stalin feel that we mean to support him without qualification and at great sacrifice."[89]

Chapter 8: Growth of Empire in the Modern Age 99

- "Of one thing I am certain; Stalin is not an imperialist."[90]
- As Stalin had studied for the priesthood, Roosevelt observed, "something entered into his nature of the way in which a Christian gentleman should behave."[91]
- And to Churchill, Roosevelt wrote, "I hope you will not mind my being totally frank when I tell you I think I can personally handle Stalin better than either your foreign office or my State Department. Stalin hates the guts of all your people. He thinks he likes me better, and I hope he will continue to do so.[92]

With that approach established as policy toward the Soviet Union, a systematic cleansing of anti-Stalin career executives at the U.S. Department of State was conducted that led to dismissal of Admiral William Standley, ambassador to the USSR; retirement of Soviet expert and chief of the Soviet section, Loy Henderson; and removal of Undersecretary of State Joseph Grew.[93]

When the Truman administration, on advice of pro-Soviet State Department advisors,[94] chose not to support the nationalist regime of Chiang Kai-shek in what communist sympathizers argued was a civil war waged by traditional combatants, Truman watched passively as Mao Tse-tung established a totalitarian regime in China. That gave Republicans a campaign issue: the Republicans asked, "Who lost China?"

Woodrow Wilson's ideology drew a line in civil society between forces inspired by the Wilsonian idealism of international law and international tribunals (the League of

Nations; United Nations) that replaced balance of power politics, and those who thought in terms of the national interest and national sovereignty. A fateful meeting of Allies Churchill, Stalin, and FDR, at Yalta in February 1945 granted the Soviet Union hegemony in East and Central Europe.

In Asia, in 1949, Mao Tse-tung led a communist takeover of the Republic of China. The invasion of South Korea by a communist regime in the north led by Kim Il Sung in June 1950, and a Chinese communist invasion in November 1950 of South Korea, found post-World War II America unprepared for a land war in Asia.

At age seventy, General Douglas MacArthur thought he could administer his duties from Tokyo and never spent a night in Korea. American officers posted in Korea were not well-suited for a coming war, troops were poorly equipped, and, after the successful invasion of the north at Inchon, MacArthur pushed American forces toward the Yalu, believing either that the Chinese under Mao Tse-tung would do nothing or he would be authorized to use the atom bomb against Mao's invaders. MacArthur was too settled in his ways and methods of control. His staff was composed of sycophants who controlled information that the general was given and tailored it to what MacArthur wanted to be told, and MacArthur misjudged the depth of President Truman's commitment to Wilsonian idealism.

President Truman removed MacArthur from his command in Japan but failed to educate the American people that the United States was at war with totalitarianism in North Korea *and* the People's Republic of China.

Chapter 8: Growth of Empire in the Modern Age

Anti-Communism

That ushered in the anti-communist movement as a domestic political force in American politics and led to the election of the first Republican president since Herbert Hoover, the former allied commander of the forces that won World War II, five-star General Dwight D. Eisenhower. As I mentioned earlier, the failures of Eisenhower's immediate successors, John F. Kennedy at the Bay of Pigs and Berlin, and Lyndon Johnson and Richard Nixon in Vietnam, again revealed the weakness of Wilsonian idealism and established a pattern of internationalism in American politics that had been in development since 1915.

The United States was in transition into an empire from a democratic republic. Teddy Roosevelt's assumption to the office of president after the assassination of President William McKinley in 1901 opened the door to the power of the Progressives.

From Theodore Roosevelt through the election of President Franklin Roosevelt, a pattern of foreign policy developed: imperial acts of war, followed by a struggle for economic recovery in peacetime, followed by instability brought about by war.

That may be seen in this series of presidents:

- President Harry Truman and the Korean War
- President John F. Kennedy and the Cold War
- Presidents Lyndon Johnson, Richard Nixon, and the war in Vietnam

Three successive presidents struggled to heal the economic and civic wounds of the war in Vietnam only to find the pull of imperial war too attractive to resist by Presidents William Clinton (Bosnia) and George H. W. Bush and George W. Bush (Iraq).

After the Cold War

George W. Bush, unlike his father, George H. W. Bush, experienced a religious conversion that enabled him to overcome addictions that threatened to destroy his life. Though belief in a literal interpretation of the millennium by George W. Bush cannot be confirmed, a mixture of Wilsonian idealism and immanentist religious eschatology in the foreign policy of his administration may be attributed to the influence of an obscure graduate of Wheaton University.

Michael J. Gerson had been working as a journalist at *U.S. News and World Report* when called to Austin, Texas, for an interview with then Texas Governor George W. Bush. Gerson relates that Bush told him that he had read his writings and wanted him to start as speechwriter for Bush's campaign for president. Bush had obviously spotted a similarity in Gerson to his own experience of having been "born again," and Gerson became an important influence on the policies of the second Bush administration.

Though Gerson disavows that he or President Bush affirm a belief in millenarianism,[95] Gerson's history of that administration, titled *Heroic Conservatism*, is replete with statements justifying the use of American might to redeem the world.

Taking the Declaration of Independence seriously introduces into conservatism a radical belief in the rights of every individual, and a conviction that government must act, when appropriate to secure those rights when they are assaulted by oppression, poverty and disease.[96]

Our goal is to move regimes toward political pluralism, without destructive destabilization. This is not a reckless undertaking; it is an unavoidable one. It calls for steady purpose, not mood swings of elation and despair. But there must be a sense of urgency. The question is not: are we pushing for reform too early? A different question hangs over America and the world: are we pushing for reform too late?[97]

Those who bet on the durability of the current order in the Middle East are not "realists"; they are in denial. And the only serious alternatives to that order are, on the one hand, the disciplined and ruthless forces of radical Islam and, on the other hand, the scattered forces of democracy and reform.[98]

Gerson rejects the assertion that his identification of himself and his president with the will of God is "messianic arrogance."[99] Whether Gerson's musings reflect a traditional belief in Providence or a Gnostic heresy is a question that is important because Gerson fashioned the words spoken by an American president whose policies destroyed the Republican Party.

The foreign policy failures and deficit spending of the George W. Bush administration, destroyed the Republican "brand" that was the result of those policies and so seriously disrupted American politics that a condition of disorder and weakness in civil society was revealed.

Beginning with the presidential administration of Woodrow Wilson, and exacerbated by the Great Depression, a vast, intrusive, centralized, bureaucratically administered state has taken control of government in the United States. That has an effect on American character as government service became plentiful. Whereas before, private careers in business or the professions were chosen, the stability and especially the benefits of government service became more attractive.

While previously, communities helped themselves recover from natural disasters, the first reaction of Americans today is to look for support from the national government. Risks of hurricanes and earthquakes, which can be avoided by not living on earthquake faults or on sea coasts, were ignored in the belief that the government would make good what human folly created. In politics, how presidents respond to natural disasters became tests for presidents which, if they failed, could destroy their administrations.

Moreover, an adversarial stance by American Progressives toward order, tradition, and religion has taken hold of our writers, artists, and even the poorest "educated" of our college graduates.

Centralization of power and the adversarial culture of Progressive intellectuals assure that American political culture is in decline and ripe for civil war. In the 1960s, when urban ethnics moved to the suburbs, they ceased to vote monolithically for Democrats and began to vote for Republicans. That led Richard Nixon to choose Baltimore Republican Spiro Agnew as his vice president.

A century after Wilson's second election, President Donald Trump promised working-class Democrats that he had policies that would restore manufacturing jobs and promised to protect entitlements that were their only guarantee that retirement would be secure.

Members of Congress are held in such low public opinion that the times are ripe for non-politicians to make successful appeals for elective office, though we are never quite sure what policies they will pursue.

Lack of interest in political careers by our best and brightest may be attributed to the New Class of journalists who believe they are citizens of the world and have no responsibilities as citizens of the United States.

Add to that an essential materialism that infuses American society and which Tocqueville associated with democratic regimes and we may safely conclude that American political culture today is unlike other, more exuberant, eras that defined the American people.

After the French and Indian War, American colonists became conscious of shared interests independent from the British Crown. From that came the "Spirit of '76." Other positive eras were similarly defined: World War I (the Roaring Twenties) and World War II (anti-communism) are two examples.

In 1991, the "Evil Empire" of the Soviet Union collapsed, thus releasing the energies of nations formerly subject to Russian totalitarian control. But in the United States, American political leaders were defined by peripheral personal or ideological impulses, not central political virtues.

Jimmy Carter's impious moralism, George H. W. Bush's Kennebunkport "internationalism," Bill Clinton's rapacious sexual appetite, George W. Bush's recovery from addiction and democratic idealism and, of course, Donald J. Trump's "celebrity" defined the office of the president of the United States. We would not be citizens of a democracy if we didn't ask, "What next?"

That question reveals some difficult problems: the ranks of congressional leaders are composed of the lackluster, the cunning, zealots, and utopian socialist politicians. None exist that gives confidence that after the next election we'll find anything better.

From the revolutionary era's Spirit of '76—which lasted through the failure of the Articles of Confederation until the founding of the Constitution of the United States in 1787, and the ratification debates in 1789—eighteenth-century American foreign policy was one of exceptionalism and non-involvement.[100] The Monroe Doctrine capped that defensiveness with a statement of resolve to defend America's interests and, by extension, the constitutional system of limited government that the American people fashioned to govern themselves, without the assistance of foreign powers. American foreign policy involved the prudential act of choosing between real possibilities and their consequences, always framed by an appreciation for the limits of America's resources, trade relations, and a young nation's inability to project power.

In the nineteenth century, from Abraham Lincoln's speech at Gettysburg and his Second Inaugural Address, through the expansionist and nascent imperialism of nineteenth-century America typified by President Theodore Roosevelt, a more robust, aggressive, and idea-oriented foreign policy developed. In some ways, nineteenth-century

Chapter 8: Growth of Empire in the Modern Age

American foreign policy can be seen as an extension of the growth of the power of the state that was the consequence of the Civil War, America's collective experience in the use of force, and the development of a military hardened by battle that foretold total war of the twentieth century.

The United States had now come of age and was poised to act in such distant places as the Philippines, Venezuela, Spain, and Mexico. Still, American foreign policy had a nineteenth-century classical character as symbolized in this passage from a letter of Theodore Roosevelt to Lord Trevelyan: "I dread the creation of a revolutionary habit and the creation of a class of people who take to disturbance and destruction as an exciting and pleasant business." [101]

Nineteenth-century American foreign policy did not represent revolutionary motivation and purpose so much as it represented a willingness to assert American power just because it was there to use. Too, the Monroe Doctrine served to remind American leaders that the United States had self-interests that were to be protected. An interest-focused foreign policy was accepted as normal, even patriotic, and is contrasted by twentieth-century American policy notions that the United States is selfless, disinterested in its particular aims, and motivated by "higher" principles than carefully formulated policies that both project and preserve American power.

A sea-change occurred in the twentieth century as Wilsonian idealism came to define American foreign policy. That foreign policy involved a radical change from previous American statecraft and reshaped how the American public views the purposes of American foreign policy. Wilsonian idealism is very much present today among our educated classes. This idealism conflicts with the practice of foreign policy by most nation-states that are motivated by the pursuit of their national interest. The motto of the United States Information Agency (1953–1999), founded after World War II, captures this sense of specialness: "Telling America's Story." Too often, America's Story is one of foreign blunders that are the result of a selfless pursuit of a New World Order of world peace.

This heritage was examined by Frank A. Ninkovich in his seminal work on American cultural diplomacy, *The Diplomacy of Ideas.* Ninkovich traced the role of internationalists like Andrew Carnegie, Elihu Root, and Columbia University's president Nicholas Murray Butler, in framing public opinion about the purposes of American foreign policy in terms of international law and those "'moral influences,' . . . as part of the progressive evolution of civilization, that were gradually, steadily in the course of centuries taking the place of brute force in the control of the affairs of men."[102]

An amalgam of Wilsonian messianism, a belief in progress, and the expectation that international agreements will shape a New World Order of eternal peace came to define America's foreign policy in the Progressive era, and the post-World War II commitment to Telling America's Story in Voice of America shortwave broadcasts.

These ideas became the hallmarks of the administrations of Franklin Delano Roosevelt, Harry S. Truman, Dwight D. Eisenhower, John F. Kennedy, Lyndon Johnson, Jimmy Carter, George H. W. Bush, William Jefferson Clinton, and Barack Obama and contributed to the foreign policy failures of those administrations.

It is important, therefore, that we understand the origins of these twentieth-century ideas about foreign policy, their enervating spirit, and their consequences for policy. We shall argue here that the only truly *revolutionary* ideology to grip the American nation, and America's thinking about itself, was inspired by Woodrow Wilson, Herbert Croly, and the Progressive internationalists who championed a New World Order that opposed the old order of balance-of-power politics.

The American Revolution was not revolutionary in the sense that modern ideologies that disrupted the world in the twentieth century are revolutionary. Woodrow Wilson's was. Progressive ideologues like Wilson sought a future world—within time—that approximated traditional Christianity's hope for peace eternal in a heavenly world. This secular, immanentist ideology successfully challenged the fundamental principles of the American regime—the philosophy of limited government of the founders of the Constitution of the United States—and transformed the American nation into a "Christ-Nation," thus placing the American people at risk to ideologies such as Nazism and Marxism.

The full magnitude of the damage done to American society by so-called Progressives has yet to be written. When that story is finally told, it will have significant consequences for American foreign policy.

The policy of containment, for example, that became the face of American foreign policy in response to communist imperialism, did not reflect America's true ability to force the Soviet Union into submission. Containment was not an outward-looking policy fashioned after careful consideration of the variety of options at America's disposal but a policy that looked inward at tensions in the American mind. Containment represented the conscious choice not to act to repel a life-force that threatened Western Civilization.

In protecting our national interests through a policy of containment, America experienced a loss of consciousness of what precisely it was fighting for, and its will to fight was thereby weakened. That weakening of resolve led to failures of will manifest in American foreign policy in Korea, Berlin, Cuba, and Vietnam. These foreign policy failures of twentieth-century American liberalism cast a pall over American politics and allowed the Republican Party to dominate presidential politics for close to a quarter century (excepting the ill-fated administration of Jimmy Carter) between the presidencies of Lyndon B. Johnson and George H. W. Bush, and assured that Ronald Reagan's exuberant, interest-oriented, foreign policy would contribute to the collapse of the Soviet Union.

If the United States is to survive a new century, the issue is not whether the Progressives' ideological expectation of a New World Order will be realized but whether American citizens living now will allow modern ideologies to shape American foreign policy in the twenty-first century.

In particular, there are two issues to contend with: (1) rejection of a moribund ideology that has weakened America's ability to respond to the challenges of global politics; and (2) shaping an intellectual alternative with a focus on the pursuit of America's national interests.

If current and future generations of American leaders do not rethink foreign policy in terms of national interest, these past ideologies will become even more fully absorbed into the American soul than they are at present. America will not

Chapter 8: Growth of Empire in the Modern Age   111

realize its potential and may well become a nation quite unlike that envisioned by the framers of American constitutional government—an instrumentality seeking a New World Order and a source of disorder in world politics.

The philosophy of limited government of the framers of the Constitution of the United States, of constitutional limits, of federalism, and a restricted executive power, constrained by the interests of the nation's representative institutions, will disappear, and this country may become something other than it is now—a revolutionary nation (not unlike the French nation of Napoleon), and a disruptive influence on the world stage, a threat to itself and to the stability and the order of traditional cultures and world politics. When that occurs, the transformation from democratic republic to empire will be complete.

If the aspiration for a New World Order, therefore, is not buried by a more robust and interest-oriented American foreign policy, American limited government, as we know it, will expire. The practical consequences of this theoretical insight in understanding contemporary American foreign policy are apparent.

As we have seen, the first, fitful steps in America's journey to becoming an empire were taken by Woodrow Wilson. Wilson created an ideology that now dominates the American soul. In doing so, he fashioned something that would transform American government from one of constitutional limits into a new form of government knowing no limits, indeed, an American Empire.

Empires inspired by redemptive ideologies lead to redemptive foreign policies; an America encumbered with that legacy entered the twenty-first century in pursuit of a New World Order.

Professor James Stoner observes that "[i]n all these matters, the aim seems to be to build up a body of world opinion and 'soft law,' which can influence and perhaps eventually even determine the legal outcomes in particular societies. Indeed, through creative lawyering... these bodies of so-called 'customary international law,' even when the treaties on which they are founded have not been ratified by the United States Senate, are starting to find their way into American courts."[103]

It should not go unnoticed that always accompanying the "lawyering" of international bodies in pursuit of the New World Order is military intervention. Stoner argues that "we need to restore a sense of the national interest to our considerations, and to restore this sense in light of universal principles." He further stresses that the principle of subsidiarity should prevail along with the linkage of individual rights with self-government. Democratic elections are not by themselves sufficient unless accompanied with constitutional government and the rule of law.

Though Norman Graebner, Richard Gamble, James Stoner, Jeremy Rabkin, Michael Ledeen, Robert Nisbet, and other scholars advocate a foreign policy rooted in reality and have tried to chart a course avoiding the treacherous revolutionary utopian waters of the internationalist New World Order, their efforts are made difficult by the absorption of Wilsonian idealism into the American soul.

Like Wilson, who as Graebner writes, "was unable to conceive of international relations except in moral terms,"[104] the American people ceased to think about foreign policy except in terms of a higher morality. Traditional ideas of liberty and equality were hypostatized—spun off from the context of the rule of law, federalism rooted in the Constitution of the United States, and historical experience—and made into parts of an American "creed." This dogmatic system of hypostatized ideas divides America today. As a result, the American people are easily attracted to appeals to American idealism. Americans easily run to support foreign wars, but just as easily run the other way when a price is paid in American treasure and blood for imposing a hypostatized liberty and equality upon an unsuspecting world. The contest between impulse and prudence involves a choice between the pursuit of American national interests or the pursuit of a New World Order by "revolution in permanence." That was the choice in Iraq and Afghanistan where our intellectual classes pushed American foreign policy into shaping those Muslim peoples toward adoption of Western democratic practices and "idealism."

The decision America must now make is whether to recognize that nations have interests or whether the national interest of the United States is served by denying the United Nations anything more than a role in providing humanitarian aid to Iraq, or anywhere else. The administration of George W. Bush decided to dominate politics in the region. At the end, it was confirmed that it did not know how to do so.

In other words, the United States decided incorrectly when it acted as an indifferent "redeemer" and intermediary for a supranational New World Order administered by the United Nations and did not decide to pursue a foreign policy rooted in pursuit of American national interest.

America's choices seem to fall into these categories: accept a secular religion that underlies the American Empire; destroy traditional mores through the imposition of the "permanently divisive social function" of Enlightenment rationality; or preserve America's national interest.

9

The Rise of American Empire

The election of Donald Trump implied a rejection of the policies of President George W. Bush (2001–2009). Cato Institute Michael Tanner finds the attitude toward the exercise of imperial power of George W. Bush in this statement: "We have a responsibility that when somebody hurts, government has got to move."[105]

George W. Bush destroyed the Republican brand of limited government and only Rand Paul and Donald Trump ran against those policies. All the other GOP candidates in 2016 drank the Bush "Kool Aid."

All of Trump's opponents in the GOP primary of 2016 offered no indication that Republican primary voters blamed Bush 43 for destroying the limited government GOP brand. Destruction of the limited-government Republican brand began when Ronald Reagan was persuaded to choose George H. W. Bush as his vice president instead of Paul Laxalt, governor of Nevada.

That gave the internationalist wing of the GOP a grasp on the future of the Republican Party. Though the elder Bush had excellent Republican credentials, few noticed that the only election he had won was a congressional seat from Harris County, Texas. Bush had been defeated twice, in 1964 and 1970, when he ran for the U.S. Senate from Texas. The reason: Texans knew that he was an import from New England and his father, Prescott Bush, was a liberal Republican senator from Connecticut.

That long history of liberal Republicanism from the Eisenhower administration through the end of the administration of Bush 43 in 2009 shaped the election of 2016.

Despite appeals by the most prominent Republican politicians who stood in the liberal wing of the GOP, Trump broke off the GOP from the internationalist wing of the Republican Party. That tradition had been established by Woodrow Wilson's imperial foreign policy that shapes the idea dominant even today that America must live up to its ideals and not seek its own national interest.

"Make America Great Again" is Trump's way of rejecting Wilsonian internationalist idealism. In addition, Donald Trump pulled a rabbit out of his hat by advocating closing down Mexican illegal immigration and reducing legal immigration to much lower levels than made possible by the 1965 Immigration Act.

Borrowing from the rhetoric of a 1960s British Conservative MP, Enoch Powell, Trump appealed to traditional Democrats who were aggrieved by policies benefitting non-Northern European immigrants.

Trump did not adopt policies that controlled government spending, however.

U.S. government spending is $4.746 trillion or 21 percent of gross domestic product (GDP) according to the Office of Management and Budget Report for FY 2020. In fiscal year 2015, the federal budget was $3.8 trillion, also about 21 percent of GDP. This ratio will increase as the economy cools and, under President Biden, we enter an era of high inflation.

Trump did nothing to lower the cost of college tuition, yet that can be achieved by taking two administrative measures: 1) employing FTC restraint of trade action against

Chapter 9: The Rise of American Empire

the six regional accrediting agencies and 2) directing those regional accrediting agencies to change the standard for accreditation that requires courses to be offered from physical classrooms.

Trump had also forsaken the GOP commitment to free trade.

Trump left entitlement spending untouched.

Trump avoided nominating appointees to federal agencies. He said we have too many people. But, he gave too much credit to men who achieve the military rank of admiral or general. Resistance to a standing army was strong during the early years of American government, and that was evident in common understanding that Cabinet agencies of the federal government should be managed by civilians.

The National Security Act of 1947 that created the Defense Department also made it a requirement that only civilians could lead the department. Service agencies were also required to be led by civilians.

Gradually, however, the appointment of former generals and admirals came into prominence. Here is a list.

- Ronald Reagan: Gen. Al Haig, Secretary of State; Gen. Colin Powell, National Security Council
- Bush 41: Gen. Brent Scowcroft, National Security Advisor
- Bush 43: Gen. Colin Powell, Secretary of State
- Barack Obama: Gen. Eric Shinseki, Veterans Affairs

The dam burst with the election of President Donald Trump who did not serve in the U.S. military but has demonstrated a loyalty to, and fondness for, former general and flag officers. Some point to President Trump's education at New York Military Academy where his parents sent him when they felt he needed to acquire discipline.

Donald Trump's affection for high rank military is visible in this list of appointees:

- Gen. James N. Mattis, Secretary of Defense
- Gen. Michael T. Flynn, first National Security Advisor
- Gen. H.R. McMaster, second National Security Advisor
- Gen. John F. Kelly, Homeland Security and Chief of Staff
- Brig. Gen. Mitchell Zais, Deputy Secretary of Education
- Rear Admiral Eric C. Jones, Military Advisor to the Secretary of Homeland Security
- Adm. Harry Harris, Ambassador to South Korea

Donald Trump hasn't read a book in fifty years. This is important because basic principles of the Trump administration were learned when Trump was a cadet at New York Military Academy.

The challenge of empire to traditional constitutional order occurs when the first response to acts of terror increases the powers of the state. The Patriot Act and the attack on Iraq by the Bush administration empowered the "war faction" in the president's party and millennial fundamentalists who saw these acts in term of the "Last Days." If elected in 2024, President Trump will be in a position to increase his imperial powers when confronting a rising Islam.

Rise of Islam

"Muslim" is the Arabic word for "submission"—those who submit to the faith of Islam found in the Koran. At the center of the Muslim world is Islam—a community that is the kingdom of God on earth. Muhammad (c. 570–632 CE) was the expositor of Islamic truth revealed to him by God through the angel Gabriel and written down in the Koran. The revealed word of God was disseminated by followers of Muhammad as far as India where the first mosque was established in 629 and through the Mughal Empire, which ruled most of the Indian subcontinent between 1526 and 1857. The Tang Dynasty (618–907 CE) found the first Muslims in China where they built the Huaisheng Mosque.

An Arab-Berber (Ummayad) army crossed from North Africa into Spain in 710 and speedily conquered most of the Iberian Peninsula, driving the Visigoth rulers into the northern mountains. In 718, a small Christian army, led by the nobleman Pelagius, defeated the caliphate's army in the mountains of northern Iberia and established a small, but independent, Christian Kingdom of Asturias. The year 718 was the beginning of a reconquest of Iberia that reached its height in a war with the Emirate of Grenada by King Ferdinand and Queen Isabella in 1482 to January 1492.

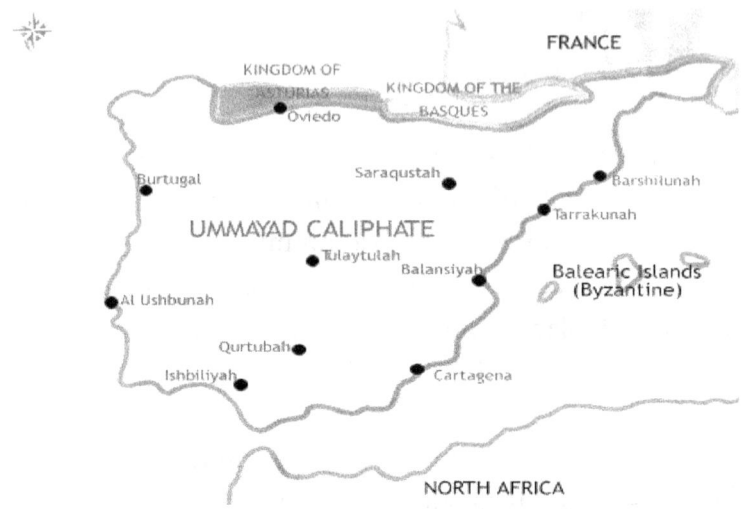

The Ottoman Empire at its peak stretched from the Caucuses, the Balkans, and Anatolia to the Middle East and North Africa. Under Suleiman the Magnificent it conquered Belgrade, Budapest, Rhodes, Algiers, and Baghdad.

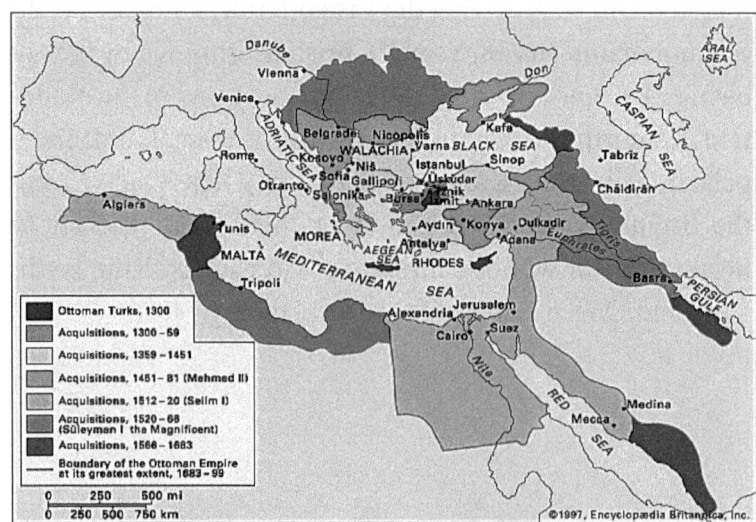

The Siege of Vienna in 1529 was the first attempt by the Ottoman Empire, led by Suleiman the Magnificent, to capture the city of Vienna, Austria. Conflict with Ottomans ranged from 1389 to 1683 and led to historic encounters between Ottoman Muslims and Christian regimes in the west.

- Battle of Kosovo (1389)
- Battle of Varna (1444)
- Conquest of Constantinople (1453)
- Capture of Belgrade (1521)
- Siege of Vienna (1529)
- Attack on Malta (1565)
- Attack on Cyprus (1571)
- Battle of Lepanto (1571)
- Siege of Vienna (1683)

Notable were four major battles, the Battle of Malta (1565), the invasion of Cyprus (1571), the Battle of Lepanto (1571), and the siege of Vienna (1683).

The siege of Vienna in 1583 signaled the pinnacle of the Ottoman Empire's power and the maximum extent of Ottoman expansion in central Europe. A second siege was waged from July 14 to early September 1683 by a vast Turkish army under the Turkish Serasker (Supreme Commander), Grand Vizier Kara Mustafa. After fending off eighteen major Turkish assaults, only a third of the originally 11,500-strong garrison in Vienna remained fit for combat, and their munitions were nearly exhausted. Responding to a call for help from Holy Roman Emperor Leopold I, imperial troops and additional forces from Saxony, Bavaria, Baden, Franconia, and Swabia, led by the king of Poland, John Sobieski, defeated Mustafa Pasha on September 11, 1683. The attack on the World Trade Towers occurred 328 years later on September 11, 2001.

Islamic radicals such as Osama bin Laden and the so-called jihadists or Islamists, which includes the al-Qaeda network and its affiliates, signify a rise of Islam motivated by a radical Islamic political religion. That political religion accepts terror and violence and is rooted in a vision of an Islamic community in this world.

In February 1998, bin Laden issued a fatwa against Jews and Crusaders. Bin Laden was not qualified to issue a fatwa, but by issuing one he sought to inform Muslims about a critical issue. His fatwa of 1998 called attention to the idea that "crimes and sins committed by the Americans are a clear declaration of war on Allah."[106]

Bin Laden's "ruling" directs Muslims that "to kill the Americans and their allies—civilians and military—is an individual duty for every Muslim who can do it in any country in which it is possible to do it, in order to liberate the al-Aqsa Mosque and the holy mosque [Mecca] from their grip, and in order for their armies to move out of all the lands of Islam, defeated and unable to threaten any Muslim. This is in accordance with the words of Almighty Allah, 'and fight the pagans all together as they fight you all together,' and 'fight them until there is no more tumult or oppression, and there prevail justice and faith in Allah.'"

Accompanying the call to kill enemies of Allah is a view that "martyrdom is a heroic act of choosing to suffer death in the cause of Allah, and that's why it's considered by most Muslim scholars as one of the greatest forms of jihad." This pronouncement was made by Sheikh Yusuf al-Qaradawi in 2004.[107]

The desire to destroy so that what is destroyed can be built anew is a temptation that disturbed the West and the Muslim world shaped by the vision of Islam. Christian millennialists and Islamic radicals equally allow a vision of transfigured reality to block out the reality of man's creaturely being. Because of the depth of this "cross-cultural" disease of the spirit, radical Islam presents to public order in the modern world the supreme challenge of a disease of the soul impermeable to rational argument.

The term "political religion," which we examined earlier, might strike some as unusual. The vast majority of Christians and Muslims piously affirm the tenets of their orthodox spiritual traditions. But intellectual and mass movements have disrupted political order throughout the history of the West. In order to understand this rise of radical Islam as a political religion, we must appreciate these movements on the level of engendering religious experience, for the terrorism of Osama bin Laden and a variety of jihadists is a spiritual disorder.

Once before, when confronted with the threat of the political religion of Marxism within Stalin's Russia, President Roosevelt was totally ignorant and made decisions whose ill effects are felt even into the twenty-first century. After the attack on 9/11, the George W. Bush administration rushed passage of the Patriot Act. In war, not only does the power of government grow but so also do acts of law and policies that later are seen to be faulty.

The overreach of the Patriot Act, which permitted vast and intrusive monitoring of communications, left a system of surveillance that in previous times would have been rejected on its face.

Taliban forces in Afghanistan led by Mullah Mohammed Omar hosted Osama bin Laden during the time he plotted the 9/11 attacks. That led to a retaliatory invasion and disbursal of Taliban from key regions. President George W. Bush decided to attack Iraq by arguing that Iraq had weapons of mass destruction. That destabilized the balance of power in that region and gave hegemony to the radical mullahs in Iran, which now is the source of weapons and terrorist activity. American forces have been stationed in the region for eighteen years. Since 2001, these engagements have cost more than $5 trillion.

Once radicals engage in terrorist acts, a policy that aims to kill and disburse them must be pursued. But there is no lack of scholarship that has identified the religious character of certain political movements. Military action cannot be deployed against spiritual disorder.

Norman Cohn's *The Pursuit of the Millennium* (1957), an analysis of medieval European religious movements, shows the similarity of these movements to the modern political phenomena of German National Socialism and Communism. These contemporary political ideologies, Cohn shows, are similar in structure to—and in some instances take inspiration from—what we today would call the fanatical, if not irrational, medieval phenomena.

J. L. Talmon's *The Origins of Totalitarian Democracy* (1960) indicates the similarity of the secular apocalyptic strain in eighteenth-century French philosophy to the chiliastic medieval phenomena. He also traces the revolutionary consequences of this political messianism in eighteenth-century France.

Albert Camus's *The Rebel* (1951) analyzes the variants of rebellion in modern speculation and the spiritual character of revolt.

Robert Tucker's *Philosophy and Myth in Karl Marx* (1961) persuasively shows the origins of the thought of Marx in the revolution in religion instituted by idealist philosophy's creation of an image of man as God.

But perhaps most important for analysis of the nature of modern political religions are the works of Eric Voegelin in which he argues that these political movements are essentially Gnostic. These works principally are *The New Science of Politics* (1952) and *Science, Politics and Gnosticism* (1959).[108]

More recently, Daniel P. Walker and Frances Yates, following the work of Paul Kristeller, have shown the influence of Renaissance Hermeticism in the formation of modern political religion.

The mystery of reality as a process of participation in the divine origin of being was experienced by the Classical Greek philosophers as a process pointing ultimately towards transfiguration of reality. Plato's concept of the turning around of the *psyche* toward the transcendent Good beyond existence and essence in his *Republic* and St. Augustine's concept of the peregrination of the city of God and the souls of men toward Christ articulate this experience. The ascent (*epanodos*)[109] of the soul to the Agathon in Platonic philosophy, just as the conversion of the soul to God of the Christian experience, articulates a transformation of the soul. Yet this experience did not occlude the simultaneous creaturely experience of the *psyche* in the world. Body which is en-souled is also psyche which is embodied. Physical, creaturely existence is reality.

In radical Islam, the creaturely world is rejected as is the humanity of man and the goodness of the world and of material existence. What is left is only the transfiguring experience of Islam.

This quest for a world in a transfigured state, but not in its present reality, is a principal formative element in the view of radical Islam.

10

Why "Thousand Year Reichs" Fall

From 1337 to 1453, France and England fought for control of France. Though we think of England as "British," William the Conqueror was from Normandy (thus the name "Norman Conquest") and memories of ties to France of English kings were fresh.

As noted earlier, a century in historical time defines what we call an "era," and the United States is well along the way in transformation of its original character as a democratic republic into an era of empire.

If an aspiring American emperor, former president Donald Trump, can call impeachment proceedings "treason," then we know that this emperor had no intention of leaving office. That, of course, is seditious, and the months between now and the 2024 presidential election may form the future course of the American Empire for a hundred years.

If the worst case possible occurs, we may enter a period of civil war similar to that experienced by Spain. You can read about what that means in my essay entitled "Prelude to Civil War: Francis Graham Wilson on Spain."[110]

Long before the Spanish Civil War (1936–1939), Spanish Traditionalist scholars warned that the ideas of the French Revolution, carried to Spain when Napoleon invaded in 1808, were captivating Spain's intellectual classes and dominating Spain's universities.

The Progressive invasion of American higher education began in the late nineteenth century and became dominant during the Great Depression when the Roosevelt administration exponentially increased the powers of the federal government. Our Hundred Years War began in 1968, and what transpires between 2024 and 2028 may decide how much freedom the American Empire permits its "subjects."

Our wealthy families have little to lose. Most are governed by second- and third-generation heirs who inherited their wealth. The "losers" will be those Americans not born into great wealth but with the desire to start new enterprises, finance them, and grow to become the next generation of Apple, Amazon, Facebook, or Netflix.

Most will assess how much financing is needed and not even try to start new companies. And those risk takers who do try will find themselves limited by local, state, and federal laws and regulations. During the next fifty years, though a remnant of conservative activists may seek deregulation and lowering of taxes, they will find empires are resistant to diminution of power.

The political consequences of this unique form of American political religion shaped by Woodrow Wilson was captured in this observation of Irving Kristol:

> [O]nce upon a time, in this country the question of democracy was a matter for political philosophy rather than for faith. And the way in which a democratic political philosophy was gradually and inexorably transformed into a democratic faith seems to me to be perhaps the most important problem in American intellectual—and ultimately political—history.[111]

Chapter 10: Why "Thousand Year Reichs" Fall

The rise of an American Empire contains five internal limitations that will contribute to its ultimate collapse.

I. The political religion of the American Empire is a nineteenth-century ideology.

Though the Wilsonian political religion still resonates with environmental activists and appears in the language of ill-educated elected leaders (and the detritus of Euro-trash culture), Wilsonian internationalism runs aground on reality. Wars are costly, and the American people pay for war with high taxes and spilled blood. After a while, they vote out of office internationalists and policies not driven by national interest.

The League of Nations, the United Nations, and all the other international organizations that the Progressives fostered, ultimately conflict with an American foreign policy grounded in the pursuit of national interest. Though internationalist rhetorical cant clutters our intellectual journals, academic fora, and media discourse with ideological concepts, the actual practice of statecraft and the pursuit of national interest ultimately prevail.

Still, the process takes time.

So deeply rooted are the internationalist aspirations of our intellectual classes that the hypostatized ideas of *democracy*—absent the rule of law; *equality*—absent a consciousness of justice; and *liberty*—absent a sense of responsibility, have become the common language of Progressives whom we now identify as politically correct elites. In light of those hypostatized ideas, historical communities must be judged to be defective, including our own nation that spawned and allows political correctness police to educate our young.

A critical reading of this passage from John F. Kennedy's Inaugural Address serves to explain this confusion in the American culture and how deep the revolution in permanence has seeped into the American soul:

> Let every nation know, whether it wishes us well or ill, that we shall pay any price, bear any burden, meet any hardship, support any friend, oppose any foe to assure the survival and the success of liberty.

To be sure, these beautiful, idealistic words were much celebrated by a generation who thought working for the state was a noble calling, but they, too, ran aground on the rock of reality.

First, it is not the liberty of the American political community that is to be defended, but liberty in general.

Second, other nations, even those friendly to American interests, are put on notice that they will be judged by the standards of an ideal liberty evoked by an arrogant American president. America's international relationships and policies will be based not on mutual interest and security, but on our friends' willingness to impose uniquely American concepts of civil liberty upon their own societies.

Third, this presidential rhetoric overestimated the capacity of American citizens to pay any price, bear any burden, meet any hardship, particularly as the toll of death of young Americans in Vietnam was tallied.

Fourth, since the revolution in permanence is destructive of traditional cultures—including our own, and should not even be sought by prudent statesmen—a skepticism about the American nation's ability to meet the exigencies of international politics (and a skepticism about politics itself) sets in. At the very moment that the American nation has been thrust into preserving the balance of power in every part of the world, America's educated classes believe that pursuing a balance of power in the world is "un-American."

Even today, otherwise intelligent Americans think of themselves as cynical when they understand that the American nation has interests and that those interests should be served. The Wilsonian secular religion has become the American political tradition, and American constitutionalism and an interest-oriented foreign policy is rejected. Conflicted by idealism posing as statecraft, the American people have become skeptical.

Wilsonian ideology of revolution in permanence *breeds* skepticism because it leads to failure, revolution, and destruction of order. In turn, skepticism leads to a vicious realism that lacks virtue. In a public arena filled with unrealizable ideals now perceived as lies, American politics yields a Richard Nixon, a Henry Kissinger, and other amoral "realists" for whom amorality provides respite from falsehood. Kissinger's defense of the government of the People's Republic of China when it suppressed China's democracy movement is an example. In reaction to the acid of that skepticism, the American electorate coughs up personages such as John F. Kennedy, Jimmy Carter, William Jefferson Clinton, and George W. Bush whose foreign policies constitute a vicious idealism absent of prudence. As a result, American foreign policy exists in tension between two poles: realism without virtue and Progressive idealism without prudence.

II. Expectation of Universal peace is not a real possibility.

St. Augustine's *The City of God* should be required reading for every educated American because it teaches us about true realism, quite different from the flawed vision of the Nixons and Kissingers of American politics. For a man who is sometimes accused of being so otherworldly that he has little to say about pragmatic political reality, St. Augustine's observations on peace are eminently practical. His civilization had collapsed, Christianity was held accountable for the collapse, and Augustine attempted to rally his fellow Christians to a consciousness of the community of the City of God.

The peace of the City of God is what you would expect of a community of men who love God. Their souls turned to God; they look forward with hope (while in the pilgrim condition of this life) to a life of eternal peace after death. In contrast, the peace of this world is fragile, easily broken, and often crueler than war. Will there be a moment in time, perhaps for a thousand years, when men will live in peace? No, St. Augustine writes. The millennium cannot be taken literally. It is but a metaphor for the age initiated with the coming of Christ that will end only with his Second Coming.

Contrast those words with the millennial visions of the New World Order, and the utopian notion that nations will turn swords into plowshares that has captivated American elites for two centuries. What is the engendering experience of this hope? Is it a lust for immortality? Since wars are not desired by reasonable men, and a world that is not at war (a New World Order from which war has been banished) is not expected by reasonable men, an element of irrationality has in effect entered intellectual culture and has become socially dominant. Seen in this context, the New World Order should be understood as the prototype of the modern rejection of the reality of our mortality and the injection of irrationality in the American soul.

The rejection of mortality, however, is only one aspect of a panoply of modern rejections including rejection of gender differences (feminism and homosexuality); rejection of aging through plastic surgery; rejection of the human tendency to pursue unhealthy things such as alcohol and smoking—and attempts to prepare for life after death through quick-freezing cryogenics. All the "New Age" Progressive nostrums are parts of a greater scheme of spiritual disorder.

III. The rule of law, political rights, and constitutional government are the antipodes of egalitarianism, universal rights, and the will to impose plebiscitary democracy on non-Western cultures.

America must preserve its commitment to justice and respect for human rights, but that commitment must be based on an articulated theory of justice and political philosophy.

The account of Creation in the first chapter of Genesis speaks of equality that is rooted in reality. The Elohim, having decided to make man "in our image" (Genesis 1:26), gives rise to the recognition that all men have an obligation to treat their fellow men with justice—as a moral obligation. Every man should be treated equally with the justice required of beings made in the image of God. But recognizing our obligation to be just is one thing. Dedicating our foreign policy to the imposition of American concepts of human rights and democracy on other countries is another.

Our guide should be Aristotle, who tried valiantly to confront the Sophistic notion that *nomos* (law) and *physis* (nature) were opposed. The Sophists, in the late stage of their development, had become moral relativists and argued that laws create principles of right or justice that have as their purpose to keep down the strong. So, the natural strength of the stronger, which of right should prevail, is opposed by the laws of the weaker, though numerically larger community of men, who fear the strong. Justice, the Sophists argued, is the will of the stronger.

Aristotle's answer, no more than two pages of his life's work, is one of the most significant contributions to the corpus of Western political theory and a theory of justice that has ennobled Western Civilization through the principle of natural law.

There is right (*dike*), Aristotle wrote, by convention. But there is also right by nature. Justice exists by law *and* by nature. Yet because what is right by nature everywhere has the same force, and because it nevertheless changes, it requires the judgment of just men to know which is which. The just man is the measure by which what is right by nature can be known. Right requires judgment, not definition.[112]

Here is stated a truth on which stability and order of all societies is grounded—the education of men is both for citizenship and for the just life. Societies are just which enable men to be good men and good citizens. This is a very simple measure by which to distinguish traditional cultures from aberrations deformed by modern ideologies.

Progressives are not guided by this truth. Instead, they are motivated to establish a world in which force has been banished, a world where nations may not seek their own national self-interest by unilateral action, and a world in which supranational organizations determine when force may be used. In fostering this myth, they absolve nations and human actors from making judgments about right and wrong, justice and injustice, peace and war. And they ignore an economy of justice by which statesmen judge whether to shed blood or not. That economy was ignored by Woodrow Wilson when, in the name of peace, he brought the twentieth century to its knees and created an imbalance of power into which stepped Lenin, Stalin, Hitler, and Mao.

IV. Underlying the imposition of hypostatized concepts of liberty, democracy, and peace on other countries is a complex of secular messianism, moral arrogance, and ignorance of political philosophy.

Self-government, from the Progressive perspective, is better than good government. Independence is better than ordered society. Self-determination thus becomes the supreme political good, and for its sake we are prepared to accept brutality. Though quite silly when looked at from some distance, the arrogance of utopian democracy is dangerous precisely because it is addled. The complex network of social interrelationships in non-Western countries is such that to impose a democratic paradigm on these subcultures is to do no more than superimpose an ideological overlay that will be fragile at best. The substance of traditional religious, social, and political order is disoriented as a result, and what order existed previously may even cease to be viable, leaving only the ideological rhetoric of democracy in which no one believes. This dilemma has faced the United States in Iraq and any other parts of the world into which American power may be projected. Once an American order is established, will it destroy traditional order? Will the virus of Enlightenment rationality carried by our academic, politically correct elites be unleashed in a fit of nation-building so destructive to traditional cultures that future generations of Americans will perish as a consequence?

It is true that it is not in our interest in the long term to impose our ideas on others because, in the end, American boys and girls will pay the price in blood, if we persist.

The feminization of the American military; the choice of female ambassadors for countries whose women are second-class citizens, the flaunting of our "right" to choose our sexual preferences, and other reflections of our cultural crackup can only lead to failed foreign policy. Instead, we should take inspiration from the Framers of the American Constitution who saw that the rule of law, of constitutional practices, and limitations on popular will and power of government were necessary in order to balance the demands of freedom and order.

V. And then, there is the willingness of Progressive internationalists to forget justice at home. The American Empire pursued by Woodrow Wilson without ignored justice at home.

Ideologies are not rooted in a profound sense of ethics, and in the pursuit of justice and truth. Western ideological system-builders always subsume ethics to "history." Woodrow Wilson, who presided over the establishment of Jim Crow, was indifferent to the plight of American Negroes.

Disenfranchisement of Blacks met with no response by Woodrow Wilson. "Jim Crow laws multiplied rapidly. Begun tentatively in the 1880s and accepted by the Supreme Court in 1896, legal segregation moved inexorably forward during the Progressive Era in state after state."[113] The American Empire sought by Woodrow Wilson was blind to the civil rights of racial minorities because it was not based on a political philosophy concerned about the order of the soul and the order of society. Justice plays no role in the revolution in permanence.

Today, apparently in gratitude to the Truman, Kennedy, and Johnson administrations' policies on civil rights, by which discrimination by government was rejected and civil rights affirmed by federal civil rights laws, Black Americans vote in lock step with those committed to a sociology of ever-increasing state power. The greater glory of the centralized, bureaucratically administered state is the knee-jerk political philosophy of America's Black leaders. Their alignment with one party, though politically astute in the short term, promises great difficulties for future generations of Black Americans. The power of the empire in future years may well be used to destroy their liberties, just as well-meaning transcendentalists affirmed them in 1865 as did Progressives in the 1960s. After fifty years of repudiation of America's racist past through the use of imperial power, it is not as clear that this same empire will not use unbridled power to impose new forms of slavery in future centuries on *all* Americans.

The link between those who favor increasing state power in domestic United States politics and those who advocate an idealistic foreign policy transcending American interests is indelible. The Progressive commitment to an internationalist foreign policy and the growth of the administrative state are linked to the Seventeenth Amendment of the Constitution of the United States. Adopted in 1913 by Progressives so as to provide for direct election of United States Senators, the great sucking sound that was heard throughout the body politic emanated from the escape of power from local governments, and state legislatures, into the federal government. At last, an institution of the federal government could be turned to the advancement of "moral causes" unmediated by non-ideologically driven motives, by special interests, and by prudential considerations.

If one examines the ideological conflicts that have torn American society apart and fueled American national politics in the 20th and 21st centuries, it will be seen that virtually all are rooted in the Progressives' politicization of the electoral process through the direct election of the United States Senate. By that means, the United States Senate became the playground of elected officials who hitch their political careers to ideological causes. The result removed state government as the focus of the most ambitious and qualified politicians. The founders expected the Senate of the United States to represent state interests, not ideologies. The Progressives arrogantly asserted in 1913 that the Founders were wrong, and thus changed the nature of American politics forever.[114] All that remains is to abolish the Electoral College and commit to an era of empire founded on plebiscitary democracy.

If that occurs, politics in the United States will lose its last connection to the limited government established at the Constitutional Convention of 1787, and a new imperial era of rule will reshape our political party system into a system controlled by American emperors.

Appendix I

James Madison, Notes of the Constitutional Convention, Annotated in Four Acts

Madison's Notes, cited here, are referenced by page numbers taken from the edition of Madison's Notes edited by James McClellan and M. E. Bradford from their annotated edition of Jonathan Elliot's Debates in the Several State Conventions, Vol. III, Debates in the Federal Convention of 1787 as Reported by James Madison. *I have presented this edition in Four Acts, as if it constituted a performance of a theatrical production. This edition was published in Richmond, Virginia, by James River Press in 1989. James River Press was created by James McClellan for the purpose of publishing the Bradford/McClellan edition of Madison's Notes. Bradford and McClellan were originalist interpreters of the Constitution of the United States. Melvin Bradford, who died in 1993, was a "Fugitive Agrarian" critic of Southern literature who taught literature at the University of Dallas. James McClellan, who died in 2005, was chief counsel and staff director of the Subcommittee on Separation of Powers of the Senate Committee on the Judiciary.*

Session I: Act I, Scenes 1–3
Major issues:
  a. Who is most important?
  b. Most important day?
  c. Who was a nationalist? States rightists?
  d. Who won? Nationalists or states rightists?
  e. Was liberty preserved?
  f. Would Senate represent state interests or people
  g. Connection between people and interests
  h. Unity or diversity
  i. Models of the new government; federalism

- j. What kind of republic do we have?
- k. Restricting or empowering document?
- I. Session One: Act I, Scenes 1–3
  - Lack of quorum
  - Democracy vs. liberty
  - Secrecy of the convention
  - Virginia Plan
  - Powers of Congress
  - Electing the executive
  - Council of Revision

p. 25 **14 May 1787**—Meeting
25 May 1787—Seven states assemble
-Washington elected president of Convention.

p. 26 -Washington "lamented his want of better qualifications."

p. 26 -Delaware can only accept a system whereby each state has only one vote like the Articles.
-Rules Committee established

p. 26 **28 May 1787**

p. 27 King and Mason: no recorded votes

p. 27 standing rules established:
-Seven states represented
-read minutes
-decorum

p. 29 Butler against publication of proceedings
29 May 1787

p. 29 Silence! Is this moral or conducive to liberty?

p. 30 Randolph introduces Virginia Plan
-Purpose?
-View of Articles? –states as jealous of this sovereignty

Appendix I: James Madison

        -Defects of Articles? –No taxation
p. 31   Virginia Plan
        #6: "force of Union against any member"
        President. And Council of Revision—can such measures ensure or nurture liberty?
p. 33   Judiciary selected by legislature
p. 33   Importance of Federalist #10 and #11
p. 34   Pickney Plan
p. 35   Charles Pickney: "abolish state governments"
p. 36   Morris's theory of power and liberty
p. 36   Just reading Mason and Sherman you would think change was imminent
p. 38   representation debate delayed; representation and liberty
p. 39   **31 May 1787**
        -Sherman raises issue of representation and human nature
p. 40   Are democracy and liberty compatible?
        -Gerry/Mason/Wilson/Madison debate
p. 41   Limits of British Influence
p. 42   Butler on scale
pp. 44-45 Madison on the nature of power
        -Do we have a restricting or empowering document?
p. 45   **I June 1787** The Executive
        -What sort of executive is needed?
        -Executive power and liberty
pp. 48-49   Exec. Term of Office
        -Is the mode of electing the exec. important?
p. 50   **2 June 1787**
p. 51   Franklin's speech: ambition and avarice
        -Issues are raised that are not resolved until 26 July

p. 57   Power or removal
p. 58   **4 June 1787**
p. 61   Executive Council

Session II: Act I, Scenes 4–6; 73–117
  Key Themes:
  - Selling the constitution to the general public and to the states
  - Madison vs. Sherman
  - Problem of scale and liberty
  - Would we be having such intensive debates if the power of the proposed government was less?
    1. Notice Gerry's remarks on p. 73. He claims that the extent and size of suffrage makes a difference. In some places when it is too small, it oppresses, but in others when it is too large, it brings in riff-raff and incompetence.
        a. Does scale matter? Does the size of the franchise really make a difference?
    2. Wilson argues on 73 that the people had parted with all necessary components of their sovereignty. What is sovereignty and why was it important where it was located?
        a. Had the people indeed parted with sovereignty?
    3. Sherman on 74 lists the objects of the Union: were these enough?
        a. Why was it better for civil and criminal matters to remain in hands of the states?

4. What is actual representation as Mason explains on 74?
5. Comparison of Madison to Sherman
   a. What is it that Madison fears the most? What about Sherman?
   b. How does Madison's views on the purpose of the Union differ from that of Sherman on p. 75?
   c. How does Madison describe the elements and components of all societies? Is his description typical of other nationalists at the Convention?
   d. Ultimately, why is Madison's acceptance of self-interest so important when compared to other delegates?
   e. Was the separation of factions a real possibility as M. believes on 76? Will Madison's prescription of size solve the problem?
   f. What other alternatives might have been better? What about reducing the overall power of the central government? Why wouldn't Madison accept this?
   g. How does Madison describe majority rule?
6. Notice Dickinson's comment about the states on p. 76. What lessons had Dickinson learned since first proposing the Articles of Confederation?

7. Was there as Wilson said on p. 77 no incompatibility between the state and national governments?
8. Madison on the Senate on p. 82. Why was it important to keep the Senate small? What did this infer about representation and scale?
9. How well does Dickinson's solar system analogy fit the kind of government being discussed here (p. 83)?
10. Looking at Gerry's speeches on 83; 85, what role did he see the states playing in protecting minority rights? Why wouldn't Madison accept this alternative?
11. P. 84: notice how the Virginians kept bringing up the issue of paper money? Why did they hope to take monetary powers away from the states? Why did they have little fear of its potential with the federal government [no real answer in debates]? Would it merely limit the number of printing presses?
12. Negative on state laws: June 8
    a. Pinckney argues states would never cooperate—that no diverse society can rely on separate parts to work together. Do we just assume this to be true? Where does this idea come from: history, ideology, experience, religion?

Appendix I: James Madison

    b. Why was the negative a cornerstone of an efficient government as Madison claimed on p. 87?
    c. Madison on centrifugal forces: 87
    d. Would a state negative eliminate or make necessary the use of force against them? How does this make for a peaceful system?
    e. Is Madison, as Gerry claims, just a "speculative projector"? p. 88
    f. Wilson vs. Bedford 88–90
        i. Why was Wilson so unwilling to codify or delineate where a state negative would operate on p. 88?
        ii. What does this say about who Wilson trusts with power and who he doesn't trust with power?
        iii. How do Wilson and Bedford approach the idea of interests differently?
        iv. Does Bedford not have good points?
    g. How does Madison react to Bedford and Gerry's arguments? Why does he panic and resort to threats of disunion? What does this say about the course of the debate—always know nationalists are losing when they do this.

      h. Patterson p. 93: what is the difference between a national and a federal government? What is being considered?
      i. On p. 95 How does Wilson defend proportional representation?
      j. P. 112–115: Randolph's Virginia Plan

Session III: Act 1, Scenes 7–9
  New Jersey or "William Patterson" Plan: 15 June 1787
- Hamilton Plan
- Decision Day of 19 June 1787

    Key Themes:
    Judiciary
    Nature of Power
    Trust
    Authorization
    Hamilton's "crisis"—real or invented
    Hamilton's basis for establishing a government
    Day of Decision

p. 115 "partly federal" plan—what does this mean?
p. 115 Patterson supported by Lansing
p. 116–18 NJ Plan; 9 resolutions
p. 116 revenue acts
p. 116 states have "original jurisdiction"
      -National court as court of appeal
p. 117 federal executive
p. 118 Judiciary
p. 118 Issue of limited supremacy of federal judiciary
p. 119 Lansing; VA plan destroys states
p. 120 States will never trust federal government
p. 121 nature of power

Appendix I: James Madison

p. 121 Congress as expensive enterprise
p. 121–24 Wilson on NJ Plan; unicameral
p. 123 Congress too powerful in NJ plan
p. 124 Randolph: NJ Plan based on coercion?

<u>18 June</u> 1787
p. 127 Hamilton Plan; he introduces plan and leaves
p. 129 Hamilton's basis for government
p. 139–45 Madison's response

Session IV: Act II, Sc. 1; 151–229
    Key Themes:
- Connection between the whole and the parts
- How does each part maintain powers of self-defense?
- How can government be partly national and partly federal?
- Two new models of government
- 2 July debate

13. Did ousting the term "national" on p. 151 make a difference?
    -Change to "the United States."
14. Lansing raises many interesting questions on 151–52. Most important might be: could a man from Georgia really be the best judge of a law in New Hampshire?
    a. Lansing on p. 153 also argues that the plan is too novel and complex. At this point in the debate, how innovative—how radical—were the plans under discussion?

15. Mason also raises many interesting questions on 154. Where did he think sovereignty lay? Was sovereignty shifted to politicians or did they merely represent it in agency? Does it really make a difference?
    a. Looking at Pennsylvania, he argues that a unicameral legislature made the people more jealous of their liberty so that they refused to grant it more power. Can it be said that too many checks and balances mislead people into losing their caution?
16. Martin claims that the general government exists to support the states, not the other way around on p. 155. Was this true? Does same thing on pp. 195–97.
17. Sherman mentions the secret committee charged with balancing the debts of the Revolution on p. 156. Rarely mentioned in debate, but crucial. Why would it make a difference if one's state was a net debtor or a net creditor?
18. Johnson on p. 159 begins to partition sovereignty. What's happening?
19. Why on p. 160 does Wilson believe the states have nothing to fear? What was he assuming about interests and unity?
20. Notice what Madison says about power on p. 161 and how it relates to scale and information. Only real threat is absence of proper

information, no inherent abuse in power per se.
21. Is there a difference between the direct and the indirect election of representatives? 163
22. Hamilton raises important question: does too frequent elections cause people to become less interested in politics? 166
23. Was it a mistake as Randolph says on p. 167 to consult popular considerations? Why were delegates better at determining right and justice and people were not?
24. Pinckney Speech
    a. on p. 178 Pinckney talks about the origins of British liberty. What occurred? How might it be replicated in a United States?
    b. Was Pinckney on 180 sensible or realistic to assume happiness was more important than defense? What would nationalists say to this?
    c. What role should foreign respect play in devising a just government? See Hamilton on 209
    d. How compatible is an empire abroad with liberty at home?
    e. How can a government be suited to the habits and genius of a people? 181
    f. Is Pinckney just a windbag?
25. Madison's speech on p. 188
    a. Must protect people from rulers, then from themselves—how so?

b. What relationship does Madison think exists between people and their interests—do people always know what is best for them? Can governing officials?
c. What kind of people is he worried about? Watch out for white trash on p. 189
d. To what extent can virtuous legislators be trusted? Will that protect minorities?
26. Hamilton claims the delegates must decide forever. Why was the issue of permanency so important? How do you make a government permanent?
27. Who does the Senate represent—Madison on 194 vs. Mason on 195.
28. Two models being debated by 28 June (p. 199)
   a. States are like individuals; state of nature, general govt guarantees rights and liberties of states
   b. States are like counties to their state government: Madison p. 199
   c. Which is more practical? Which works out the best? Which preserves liberty the most? Liberty for whom?
   d. Difference b/w treaties and a compact p. 199
   e. Why was state negative crucial to Madison's argument?

  f. What happens if govt is too weak
  g. Is there an inherent contradiction b/w sovereignty of the people and sovereignty of the states? Were the two compatible?
  h. Is the problem the idea of sovereignty? Gerry: 210
29. Interesting sidebar in middle of the impasse on 28 June: Franklin calls for prayer
  a. Good opportunity to discuss what impressions we carry with us into our study. I always had been told that Franklin told funny stories—never heard he called for prayer!
  b. What does it say that Franklin's motion never carried? Not really a religious question, but a question about the role of religious insight at the convention as well as the humility of the delegates
30. Johnson on p. 205: whole problem is definition of people w/I the states: society or societies. Could we say this is what the Phil. Convention was most concerned about? [don't ask which side won—yet.]
31. Did equality of the states in the Senate destroy the Constitution? 207
32. Baldwin: 212: would it not have been better to agree on the powers of the new government before its structure? Why did they do this????

33. On 215 Wilson discusses representation—does he offer a good defense of majority rule? How does his thought contradict Madison's
    a. with equality in the Senate? Wilson says we would have precisely what we have under the Articles. Is this true?
34. Madison on 217: Does Madison have two faces? One majoritarian; one protective of minority rights?
    a. Madison on sectionalism
    b. Is Madison's solution to slave vs. free states reasonable?
35. King vs. Bedford 220–21: is the question really about small vs. large states or landed vs. landless states?
36. King and paper security: calls for bill of states' rights 223
37. 2 July
    a. Sherman's call for compromise: CT or Great Compromise
    b. Morris: lack of info therefore need elite and not trust people 227
    c. Why did Wilson and Madison oppose a committee and compromise? Was this a ploy? 228

Session V: Act II, Scene 2
    6–20 August (p. 366–470)
- Change; amending power
- Gerry: expedience

Appendix I: James Madison 153

- Mason: accommodation
- Committee on Detail
- House checking Senate; is "negative" power good?
- Why are qualifications so important?
- Power of Congress: Is Congress given too many liberties?
- The language of liberty

p. 386 Rutledge, as chair (Committee on Detail) presents a draft of the Constitution a seven-page folio pamphlet to each member (based on many sources).

p. 366 "Supreme" bodies

p. 367 Legislative bodies checking each other
All states except Delaware and NJ upper house already called Senate.

p. 367 IX, V, and IV—-qualifications.

p. 370–371 Fundamental Change: the power of Congress. Convention was giving Congress very broad power, "indefinite power"; Committee report gives Congress 18 specific and limited powers; 7 of these from Articles.
-Six specific limitations on Congress—including treason, export duties, and migration.

p. 373 Article X–almost directly from the New York and Massachusetts constitutions.
-"President" as name of presiding officer.

p. 374 Congress in charge of the jurisdiction of the courts.

p. 375 XII; XIII/First limitations on the state

7 August Begin to debate the plan in detail.

p. 380 R. King—Legislature would not need to meet every year.
-Sherman/Mason: Legislature should meet every year at a specified time.
p. 383. States in charge of voting.
-Mason potentially defending the common man?
p. 386. -Franklin's anti-democratic rhetoric about electors.

<u>8 August</u>: Qualifications for electing members of the House
p. 387 Mercer's dislike of whole plan.

<u>9 August</u> Committee gave federal too much power in election.
p. 399 Madison as "godfather" of immigration.
p. 401 Morris's xenophobia?

<u>10 August</u> Almost all state constitutions required religious and property requirements.
-House and Senate.
<u>11 August</u> Can legislatures adjourn themselves? Freedom of speech in legislature is protected.
p. 414 Discussion of adjournment.
<u>13 August</u> All Hades breaks out over the origination of money bills.
<u>14 August</u> Who will pay for Congress?
<u>15 August</u> Veto power.
<u>16 August</u> Taxing power; "General Welfare"; and "express power"
<u>20 August</u> Necessary and Proper

Session VI: Act II, Scene 3; 289–352

Appendix I: James Madison

- Draft Constitution
- Locus of authority, powers of Congress, limits of federal supremacy
- Martin's criticisms
    38. Why was Morris opposed to granting states police powers—paper money? 290
    39. How did nationalists begin to shift on state negative? What role would the courts play—were they a better or worse alternative?
    40. Why would Sherman support judicial review and not state negative? 292
    41. Martin's proposal of a supremacy clause? Why is such a clause important? Where did he get this? 293
    42. Problems of the presidency; selection and electors 295–96
        a. Why was re-eligibility such a divisive issue?
        b. Madison insisted that judiciary and executive should be allowed to cooperate on p. 298. Why? What are the benefits and problems with this?
        c. Key question is could the courts check either branch—why such little attention to this?
    43. Is anyone struck by the nature of the debate on the judiciary? Is anything missing from this debate? What about its power?
    44. <u>19 July</u>: does Morris sufficiently defend a strong executive? 308

a. Is the president the chief guardian of the people? How so? What about other branches—what are they doing?
45. Structural issue: couldn't agree on eligibility so they move to popular election—why?
46. Madison on 317: Is he perceptive or incredibly naïve?
47. Who are electors supposed to represent? Why is their appointment so hotly debated?
48. Both sides want executive and legislative powers separated. What did they miss? What ultimately united the two? Parties!
49. Key questions on 21 July related to the "revisionary power" of the judiciary. What is this?
    a. How might revisionary power strengthen reliance on original intent: two types of original intent. 322
    b. Why has history proven Madison wrong about legislative power being vortex? 322
    c. Gerry argues judges are "statesmen"—are they merely politicians in black robes? Maybe use Pat Robertson weekend quotation: five men deciding most important issues for the people.
    d. Will judicial review destroy confidence in government as Martin argues on 324?

Appendix I: James Madison

        e. Mason: unconstitutional vs. improper laws 326
        f. Behind all this is the belief that the executive also has revisionary powers—what are they? Veto?
    50. Did it make a difference how the constitution would be ratified? 334

Session VII: Act III, Scene 1 pp. 385–94
- Role of national legislature
- Popular rule and voting
- Qualifications for voting and service

Session VIII: Act III, scene 2 pp. 470–508 (bullets differ from readings)
- Direct taxation and limits on taxing power
- Executive powers
- Election of executive
  - a. Discuss the advantages and disadvantages of supermajorities in general and on commercial policy and export taxes in particular
  - b. 477: One of the few comments on the evils of slavery—why?
  - c. Why didn't the delegates to the Phil. Convention do something about this great evil? Rutledge has the answer on 477
  - d. Mason talks about slavery on 479 as a national sin—can nations sin? What does this presuppose?
  - e. Definition of terms for militia 487

1. What was the relationship between militias and republicanism?
2. Was this a defeat for state rightists?
   f. 493: crucial question by Langdon: who judges/interprets the Constitution?
   g. More on election of the president
   h. Problems of debt holders and public debt

Session IX: Act III, Scene 3; 508–39 (27–31 August)
- Executive and military
- Judicial powers
- Commerce and liberty
- Expandability of the regime
- Proper role of judiciary in a republic?
- Is judicial restraint conducive to preserving liberty?
- Must states be restrained?
- Is "Madisonian" regulation a key to liberty?

p. 510 Pickney—problem of large salaries for judiciary.
p. 511 Madison: Does he support judicial restraint?
   -Issue of judicial impeachment postponed.
pp. 510-512 Could the U.S. sue a state? Consider *U.S. v. Texas* (1892).
p. 512 Sherman's "gift" of judicial power.
<u>28 August</u> Restrictions on states.
p. 516 Madison's hyperbole
p. 517 No fugitive slave provision
<u>29 August</u>: Regulation of commerce; export duties; and slavery compromise
   1-Taxation most important; 2) Regulation of commerce nearly as important.

Appendix I: James Madison

p. 519 Pickney on state power
p. 522 Madison's paean to the regulation of trade
p. 523 Gorham on regional harmony
p. 525 Morris: adopting new states; Luther Martin's response.
p. 527 Williamson on the giving of Western lands.
p. 528 Luther Martin again "morphing"
p. 531 Amnesty Clause voted down; resolved 12 Sept.
<u>31 August</u> Ratification

Session X: Act IV, Scene 1; 539–599
- Ambiguity of common defense and general welfare
- Uniformity of congressional legislation
- Electing president and role of president
- Presidential powers
    i. Electoral college
        1. Who elects the president of the United States?
    j. Morris claims on p. 546 this was an attempt to remove "cabal"—why did it fail?
        1. Was electoral college really capable of doing this even w/o parties forming in 1790s
    k. What was wrong with having Senate elect the president if Electoral College failed to give majority?
    l. 549—take liberty to go off on a tangent. Why would they want to encourage patents? Was this not a special privilege that might extinguish liberty and entrepreneurship

1. Whose interests are being served? Entrepreneur or general consumers
m. 551-2: was there any merit to the suspicion that the president would usually be the minority candidate?
n. 560: who elects president? STATES
o. Is the question on presidential election a contest b/w nationalists and states rightists, or are there deeper divisions at work here?
p. What happens to Edmund Randolph? Can anyone explain his shift? See also 578 and 581—this is an important question b/c both he and Gerry arrived at Philadelphia as strong nationalists. What does their shift reveal about the Convention?
q. Discuss very nationalistic letter accompanying the Constitution on 594
r. Mason and Bill of Rights 599

Session XI: Act IV, Scene 2 (13–17 September, pp. 599–624)
- Representation and liberty as central issues
- Appointment power of pres.
- Amending process
- Dissent vs. popular rule and liberty
- Refusal of three to sign: Randolph, Gerry, and Mason
- Committee on Style
- Congressional power—is more representation really better?

<u>13 Sept.</u>
p. 599 Mason on sumptuary regulations.

Appendix I: James Madison   161

p. 600 Mason on state duties; taxation and duties
p. 601 Committee on Style revisions on Ratification.
<u>14 Sept.</u>
p. 602   Williamson on number of house members; at least two per state
p. 603 Madison: President always dependent on legislature -allow impeached president to remain in office.
p.603   Baldwin on congressional "double dipping"
p. 604 appointive power
p. 605 Sherman: First case against internal improvements -Wilson-states obstructing general welfare.
p. 606 Madison and Pickney want national university
p. 608 Secrecy/public acknowledgement of debt.
14 Sept. Congressional powers proposed, but rejected
17 Sept.
pp. 618-619   Franklin on infallibility
        -"politics of muddling through"
p. 620 Washington's speech
p. 622 Blount signs after saying he will not
p. 622 Gerry as Prophet
p. 623 King and secrecy

Session XII: Final Reflections

Appendix II

Port Huron Statement
Introduction: Agenda for a Generation (abridged)

We are people of this generation, bred in at least modest comfort, housed now in universities, looking uncomfortably to the world we inherit.

When we were kids the United States was the wealthiest and strongest country in the world; the only one with the atom bomb, the least scarred by modern war, an initiator of the United Nations that we thought would distribute Western influence throughout the world. Freedom and equality for each individual, government of, by, and for the people— these American values we found good, principles by which we could live as men. Many of us began maturing in complacency.

As we grew, however, our comfort was penetrated by events too troubling to dismiss. First, the permeating and victimizing fact of human degradation, symbolized by the Southern struggle against racial bigotry, compelled most of us from silence to activism. Second, the enclosing fact of the Cold War, symbolized by the presence of the Bomb, brought awareness that we ourselves, and our friends, and millions of abstract "others" we knew more directly because of our common peril, might die at any time. We might deliberately ignore, or avoid, or fail to feel all other human problems, but not these two, for these were too immediate and crushing in their impact, too challenging in the demand that we as individuals take the responsibility for encounter and resolution.

While these and other problems either directly oppressed us or rankled our consciences and became our own subjective concerns, we began to see complicated and disturbing paradoxes in our surrounding America. The declaration "all men are created equal . . ." rang hollow before the facts of Negro life in the South and the big cities of the North. The proclaimed peaceful intentions of the United States contradicted its economic and military investments in the Cold War status quo.

We witnessed, and continue to witness, other paradoxes. With nuclear energy whole cities can easily be powered, yet the dominant nation-states seem more likely to unleash destruction greater than that incurred in all wars of human history. Although our own technology is destroying old and creating new forms of social organization, men still tolerate meaningless work and idleness. While two-thirds of mankind suffers undernourishment, our own upper classes revel amidst superfluous abundance. Although world population is expected to double in forty years, the nations still tolerate anarchy as a major principle of international conduct and uncontrolled exploitation governs the sapping of the earth's physical resources. Although mankind desperately needs revolutionary leadership, America rests in national stalemate, its goals ambiguous and tradition-bound instead of informed and clear, its democratic system apathetic and manipulated rather than "of, by, and for the people."

Not only did tarnish appear on our image of American virtue, not only did disillusion occur when the hypocrisy of American ideals was discovered, but we began to sense that what we had originally seen as the American Golden Age was actually the decline of an era. The worldwide outbreak of revolution against colonialism and imperialism, the entrenchment of totalitarian states, the menace of war, overpopulation, international disorder, super technology—these trends were testing the tenacity of our own commitment to democracy and freedom and our abilities to visualize their application to a world in upheaval.

Our work is guided by the sense that we may be the last generation in the experiment with living. But we are a minority—the vast majority of our people regard the temporary equilibriums of our society and world as eternally functional parts. In this is perhaps the outstanding paradox; we ourselves are imbued with urgency, yet the message of our society is that there is no viable alternative to the present. Beneath the reassuring tones of the politicians, beneath the common opinion that America will "muddle through," beneath the stagnation of those who have closed their minds to the future, is the pervading feeling that there simply are no alternatives, that our times have witnessed the exhaustion not only of Utopias, but of any new departures as well. Feeling the press of complexity upon the emptiness of life, people are fearful of the thought that at any moment things might be thrust out of control. They fear change itself, since change might smash whatever invisible framework seems to hold back chaos for them now. For most Americans, all crusades are suspect, threatening. The fact that each individual sees apathy in his fellows perpetuates the common reluctance to organize for change. The dominant institutions are complex enough to blunt the minds of their potential critics, and entrenched enough to swiftly dissipate or entirely repel the energies of protest and reform, thus limiting human expectancies. Then, too, we are a materially improved society, and by our own improvements we seem to have weakened the case for further change.

Some would have us believe that Americans feel contentment amidst prosperity—but might it not better be called a glaze above deeply felt anxieties about their role in the new world? And if these anxieties produce a developed indifference to human affairs, do they not as well produce a yearning to believe that there *is* an alternative to the present, that something *can* be done to change circumstances in the school, the workplaces, the bureaucracies, the government? It is to this latter yearning, at once the spark and engine of change, that we direct our present appeal. The search for truly democratic alternatives to the present, and a commitment to social experimentation with them, is a worthy and fulfilling human enterprise, one which moves us and, we hope, others today. On such a basis do we offer this document of our convictions and analysis: as an effort in understanding and changing the conditions of humanity in the late twentieth century, an effort rooted in the ancient, still unfulfilled conception of man attaining determining influence over his circumstances of life.

Values

Making values explicit—an initial task in establishing alternatives—is an activity that has been devalued and corrupted. The conventional moral terms of the age, the politician moralities—"free world," "people's democracies"—reflect realities poorly, if at all, and seem to function more as ruling myths than as descriptive principles. But neither has our experience in the universities brought us moral enlightenment. Our professors and administrators sacrifice controversy to public relations; their curriculums change more slowly than the living events of the world; their skills and silence are purchased by investors in the arms race; passion is called unscholastic. The questions we might want raised—what is really important? can we live in a different and better way? if we wanted to change society, how would we do it?—are not thought to be questions of a "fruitful, empirical nature," and thus are brushed aside.

Unlike youth in other countries we are used to moral leadership being exercised and moral dimensions being clarified by our elders. But today, for us, not even the liberal and socialist preachments of the past seem adequate to the forms of the present. Consider the old slogans: Capitalism Cannot Reform Itself, United Front Against Fascism, General Strike, All Out on May Day. Or, more recently, No Cooperation with Commies and Fellow Travelers, Ideologies Are Exhausted, Bipartisanship, No Utopias. These are incomplete, and there are few new prophets. It has been said that our liberal and socialist predecessors were plagued by vision without program, while our own generation is plagued by program without vision. All around us there is astute grasp of method, technique—the committee, the ad hoc group, the lobbyist, the hard and soft sell, the make, the projected image—but, if pressed critically, such expertise is incompetent to explain its implicit ideals. It is highly fashionable to identify oneself by old categories, or by naming a respected political figure, or by explaining "how we would vote" on various issues.

Theoretic chaos has replaced the idealistic thinking of old—and, unable to reconstitute theoretic order, men have condemned idealism itself. Doubt has replaced hopefulness—and men act out a defeatism that is labeled realistic. The decline of utopia and hope is in fact one of the defining features of social life today. The reasons are various: the dreams of the older left were perverted by Stalinism and never re-created; the congressional stalemate makes men narrow their view of the possible; the specialization of human activity leaves little room for sweeping thought; the horrors of the twentieth century symbolized in the gas ovens and concentration camps and atom bombs, have blasted hopefulness. To be idealistic is to be considered apocalyptic, deluded. To have no serious aspirations, on the contrary, is to be "tough-minded."

In suggesting social goals and values, therefore, we are aware of entering a sphere of some disrepute. Perhaps matured by the past, we have no formulas, no closed theories—but that does not mean values are beyond discussion and tentative determination. A first task of any social movement is to convince people that the search for orienting theories and the creation of human values is complex but worthwhile. We are aware that to avoid platitudes we must analyze the concrete conditions of social order. But to direct such an analysis we must use the guideposts of basic principles. Our own social values involve conceptions of human beings, human relationships, and social systems.

We regard men as infinitely precious and possessed of unfulfilled capacities for reason, freedom, and love. In affirming these principles we are aware of countering perhaps the dominant conceptions of man in the twentieth century:

that he is a thing to be manipulated, and that he is inherently incapable of directing his own affairs. We oppose the depersonalization that reduces human being to the status of things—if anything, the brutalities of the twentieth century teach that means and ends are intimately related, that vague appeals to "posterity" cannot justify the mutilations of the present. We oppose, too, the doctrine of human incompetence because it rests essentially on the modern fact that men have been "competently" manipulated into incompetence—we see little reason why men cannot meet with increasing skill the complexities and responsibilities of their situation, if society is organized not for minority, but for majority, participation in decision-making.

Men have unrealized potential for self-cultivation, self-direction, self-understanding, and creativity. It is this potential that we regard as crucial and to which we appeal, not to the human potentiality for violence, unreason, and submission to authority. The goal of man and society should be human independence: a concern not with image of popularity but with finding a meaning in life that is personally authentic; a quality of mind not compulsively driven by a sense of powerlessness, nor one which unthinkingly adopts status values, nor one which represses all threats to its habits, but one which has full, spontaneous access to present and past experiences, one which easily unites the fragmented parts of personal history, one which openly faces problems which are troubling and unresolved; one with an intuitive awareness of possibilities, an active sense of curiosity, an ability and willingness to learn.

This kind of independence does not mean egotistic individualism—the object is not to have one's way so much as it is to have a way that is one's own. Nor do we deify man—we merely have faith in his potential.

Human relationships should involve fraternity and honesty. Human interdependence is contemporary fact; human brotherhood must be willed, however, as a condition of future survival and as the most appropriate form of social relations. Personal links between man and man are needed, especially to go beyond the partial and fragmentary bonds of function that bind men only as worker to worker, employer to employee, teacher to student, American to Russian.

Loneliness, estrangement, isolation describe the vast distance between man and man today. These dominant tendencies cannot be overcome by better personnel management, nor by improved gadgets, but only when a love of man overcomes the idolatrous worship of things by man. As the individualism we affirm is not egoism, the selflessness we affirm is not self-elimination. On the contrary, we believe in generosity of a kind that imprints one's unique individual qualities in the relation to other men, and to all human activity. Further, to dislike isolation is not to favor the abolition of privacy; the latter differs from isolation in that it occurs or is abolished according to individual will.

We would replace power rooted in possession, privilege, or circumstance by power and uniqueness rooted in love, reflectiveness, reason, and creativity. As a social system we seek the establishment of a democracy of individual participation, governed by two central aims: that the individual share in those social decisions determining the quality and direction of his life; that society be organized to encourage independence in men and provide the media for their common participation.

In a participatory democracy, the political life would be based in several root principles:

- that decision-making of basic social consequence be carried on by public groupings;
- that politics be seen positively, as the art of collectively creating an acceptable pattern of social relations;
- that politics has the function of bringing people out of isolation and into community, thus being a necessary, though not sufficient, means of finding meaning in personal life;
- that the political order should serve to clarify problems in a way instrumental to their solution; it should provide outlets for the expression of personal grievance and aspiration; opposing views should be organized so as to illuminate choices and facilitate the attainment of goals; channels should be commonly available to relate men to knowledge and to power so that private problems—from bad recreation facilities to personal alienation—are formulated as general issues.

The economic sphere would have as its basis the principles:

- that work should involve incentives worthier than money or survival. It should be educative, not stultifying; creative, not mechanical; self-directed, not manipulated, encouraging indepen-

dence, a respect for others, a sense of dignity, and a willingness to accept social responsibility, since it is this experience that has crucial influence on habits, perceptions and individual ethics;
- that the economic experience is so personally decisive that the individual must share in its full determination;
- that the economy itself is of such social importance that its major resources and means of production should be open to democratic participation and subject to democratic social regulation.

Like the political and economic ones, major social institutions—cultural, educational, rehabilitative, and others—should be generally organized with the well-being and dignity of man as the essential measure of success.

In social change or interchange, we find violence to be abhorrent because it requires generally the transformation of the target, be it a human being or a community of people, into a depersonalized object of hate. It is imperative that the means of violence be abolished and the institutions—local, national, international—that encourage non-violence as a condition of conflict be developed.

These are our central values, in skeletal form. It remains vital to understand their denial or attainment in the context of the modern world.

The Students

In the last few years, thousands of American students demonstrated that they at least felt the urgency of the times. They moved actively and directly against racial injustices, the threat of war, violations of individual rights of conscience, and, less frequently, against economic manipulation. They succeeded in restoring a small measure of controversy to the campuses after the stillness of the McCarthy period. They succeeded, too, in gaining some concessions from the people and institutions they opposed, especially in the fight against racial bigotry.

The significance of these scattered movements lies not in their success or failure in gaining objectives—at least, not yet. Nor does the significance lie in the intellectual "competence" or "maturity" of the students involved—as some pedantic elders allege. The significance is in the fact that students are breaking the crust of apathy and overcoming the inner alienation that remain the defining characteristics of American college life.

If student movements for change are still rarities on the campus scene, what is commonplace there? The real campus, the familiar campus, is a place of private people, engaged in their notorious "inner emigration." It is a place of commitment to business-as-usual, getting ahead, playing it cool. It is a place of mass affirmation of the Twist, but mass reluctance toward the controversial public stance. Rules are accepted as "inevitable," bureaucracy as "just circumstances," irrelevance as "scholarship," selflessness as "martyrdom," politics as "just another way to make people, and an unprofitable one, too."

Almost no students value activity as citizens. Passive in public, they are hardly more idealistic in arranging their private lives: Gallup concludes they will settle for "low success, and won't risk high failure." There is not much willingness to take risks (not even in business), no setting of dangerous goals, no real conception of personal identity except one manufactured in the image of others, no real urge for personal fulfillment except to be almost as successful as the very successful people. Attention is being paid to social status (the quality of shirt collars, meeting people, getting wives or husbands, making solid contacts for later on); much, too, is paid to academic status (grades, honors, the med school rat race). But neglected generally is real intellectual status, the personal cultivation of the mind.

"Students don't even give a damn about the apathy," one has said. Apathy toward apathy begets a privately constructed universe, a place of systematic study schedules, two nights each week for beer, a girl or two, and early marriage; a framework infused with personality, warmth, and under control, no matter how unsatisfying otherwise.

Under these conditions university life loses all relevance to some. Four hundred thousand of our classmates leave college every year.

The accompanying "let's pretend" theory of student extracurricular affairs validates student government as a training center for those who want to live their lives in political pretense, and discourages initiative from the more articulate, honest, and sensitive students. The bounds and style of controversy are delimited before controversy begins. The university "prepares" the student for "citizenship" through perpetual rehearsals and, usually, through emasculation of what creative spirit there is in the individual.

The academic life contains reinforcing counterparts to the way in which extracurricular life is organized. The academic world is founded on a teacher-student relations analogous to the parent-child relation which characterizes *in loco parentis*. Further, academia includes a radical separation of the student from the material of study. That which is studies, the social reality, is "objectified" to sterility, dividing the student from life—just as he is restrained in active involvement by the deans controlling student government. The specialization of function and knowledge, admittedly necessary to our complex technological and social structure, has produced an exaggerated compartmentalization of study and understanding. This has contributed to an overly parochial view, by faculty, of the role of its research and scholarship; to a discontinuous and truncated understanding, by students, of the surrounding social order; and to a loss of personal attachment, by nearly all, to the worth of study as a humanistic enterprise.

There is, finally, the cumbersome academic bureaucracy extending throughout the academic as well as the extracurricular structures, contributing to the sense of outer complexity and inner powerlessness that transforms the honest searching of many students to a ratification of convention and, worse, to a numbness to present and future catastrophes. The size and financing systems of the university enhance the permanent trusteeship of the administrative bureaucracy, their power leading to a shift within the university toward the value standards of business and the administrative mentality. Huge foundations and other private financial interests shape the under financed colleges and universities, making them not only more commercial, but less disposed to diagnose society critically, less open to dissent. Many social and physical scientists, neglecting the liberating heritage of higher learning, develop "human relations" or "morale-producing" techniques for the corporate economy, while others exercise their intellectual skills to accelerate the arms race.

Tragically, the university could serve as a significant source of social criticism and an initiator of new modes and molders of attitudes. But the actual intellectual effect of the college experience is hardly distinguishable from that of any other communications channel—say, a television set—passing on the stock truths of the day. Students leave college somewhat more "tolerant" than when they arrived, but basically unchallenged in their values and political orientations. With administrators ordering the institution, and faculty the curriculum, the student learns by his isolation to accept elite rule within the university, which prepares him to accept later forms of minority control. The real function of the educational system—as opposed to its more rhetorical function of "searching for truth"—is to impart the key information and styles that will help the student get by, modestly but comfortably, in the big society beyond.

The Society Beyond

Look beyond the campus, to America itself. That student life is more intellectual, and per-haps more comfortable, does not obscure the fact that the fundamental qualities of life on the campus reflect the habits of society at large. The fraternity president is seen at the junior man-ager levels; the sorority queen has gone to Grosse Pointe; the serious poet burns for a place, any place, to work; the once-serious and never-serious poets work at the advertising agencies. The desperation of people threatened by forces about which they know little and of which they can say less; the cheerful emptiness of people "giving up" all hope of changing things; the faceless ones polled by Gallup who listed "international affairs" fourteenth on their list of "problems" but who also expected thermonuclear war in the next few years; in these and other forms, Americans are in withdrawal from public life, from any collective effort at directing their own affairs.

Some regard these national doldrums as a sign of healthy approval of the established or-der—but is it approval by consent or manipulated acquiescence? Others declare that the people are withdrawn because compelling issues are fast disappearing—perhaps there are fewer bread lines in America, but is Jim Crow gone, is there enough work and work more fulfilling, is world war a diminishing threat, and what of the revolutionary new peoples? Still others think the national quietude is a necessary consequence of the need for elites to resolve complex and specialized problems of modern industrial society—but then, why should business elites help decide foreign policy, and who controls the elites anyway, and are they solving mankind's problems? Others, finally, shrug knowingly and announce that full democracy never worked anywhere in the past—but why lump qualitatively different civilizations together, and how can a social or-der work well if its best thinkers are skeptics, and is man really doomed forever to the domination of today?

There are now convincing apologies for the contemporary malaise. While the world tumbles toward the final war, while men in other nations are trying desperately to alter events, while the very future qua future is uncertain—America is without community impulse, without the inner momentum necessary for an age when societies cannot successfully perpetuate themselves by their military weapons, when democracy must be viable because of its quality of life, not its quantity of rockets.

The apathy here is, first, subjective—the felt powerlessness of ordinary people, the resignation before the enormity of events. But subjective apathy is encouraged by the objective Ameri-can situation—the actual structural separation of people from power, from relevant knowledge, from pinnacles of decision-making. Just as the university influences the student way of life, so do major social institutions create the circumstances in which the isolated citizen will try hopelessly to understand his world and himself.

The very isolation of the individual—from power and community and ability to aspire—means the rise of a democracy without publics. With the great mass of people structurally re-mote and psychologically hesitant with respect to democratic institutions, those institutions themselves attenuate and become, in the fashion of the vicious circle, progressively less accessible to those few who aspire to serious participation in social affairs. The vital democratic connection between community and leadership, between the mass and the several elites, has been so wrenched and perverted that disastrous policies go unchallenged time and again. . . .

The University and Social Change

There is perhaps little reason to be optimistic about the above analysis. True, the Dixiecrat-GOP coalition is the weakest point in the dominating complex of corporate, military, and political power. But the civil rights, peace, and student movements are too poor and socially slighted, and the labor movement too quiescent, to be counted with enthusiasm. From where else can power and vision be summoned? We believe that the universities are an overlooked seat of influence.

First, the university is located in a permanent position of social influence. It's educational function makes it indispensable and automatically makes it a crucial institution in the formation of social attitudes. Second, in an unbelievably complicated world, it is the central institution for organizing, evaluating, and transmitting knowledge. Third, the extent to which academic re-sources presently are used to buttress immoral social practice is revealed, first, by the extent to which defense contracts make the universities engineers of the arms race. Too, the use of mod-ern social science as a manipulative tool reveals itself in the "human relations" consultants to the modern corporations, who introduce trivial sops to give laborers feelings of "participation" or "belonging," while actually deluding them in order to further exploit their labor. And, of course, the use of motivational research is already infamous as a manipulative aspect of American politics. But these social uses of the universities' resources also demonstrate the unchangeable reliance by men of power on the men and storehouses of knowledge: this makes the university functionally tied to society in new ways, revealing new potentialities, new levers for change. Fourth, the university is the only mainstream institution that is open to participation by individuals of nearly any viewpoint.

These, at least, are facts, no matter how dull the teaching, how paternalistic the rules, how irrelevant the research that goes on. Social relevance, the accessibility to knowledge, and internal openness—these together make the university a potential base and agency in a movement of social change.

1. Any new left in America must be, in large measure, a left with real intellectual skills, committed to deliberativeness, honesty, reflection as working tools. The university permits the political life to be an adjunct to the academic one, and action to be informed by reason.
2. A new left must be distributed in significant social roles throughout the country. The universities are distributed in such a manner.
3. A new left must consist of younger people who matured in the postwar world, and partially be directed to the recruitment of younger people. The university is an obvious be-ginning point.
4. A new left must include liberals and socialists, the former for their relevance, the latter for their sense of thoroughgoing reforms in the system. The university is a more sensible place than a political party for these two traditions to begin to discuss their differences and look for political synthesis.
5. A new left must start controversy across the land, if national policies and national apathy are to be

reversed. The ideal university is a community of controversy, within itself and in its effects on communities beyond.

6. A new left must transform modern complexity into issues that can be understood and felt close up by every human being. It must give form to the feelings of helplessness and indifference, so that people may see the political, social, and economic sources of their private troubles, and organize to change society. In a time of supposed prosperity, moral complacency, and political manipulation, a new left cannot rely on only aching stomachs to be the engine force of social reform. The case for change, for alternatives that will involve uncomfortable personal efforts, must be argued as never before. The university is a relevant place for all of these activities.

But we need not indulge in illusions: the university system cannot complete a movement of ordinary people making demands for a better life. From its schools and colleges across the nation, a militant left might awaken its allies, and by beginning the process towards peace, civil rights, and labor struggles, reinsert theory and idealism where too often reign confusion and political barter. The power of students and faculty united is not only potential; it has shown its actuality in the South, and in the reform movements of the North.

The bridge to political power, though, will be built through genuine cooperation, locally, nationally, and internationally, between a new left of young people and an awakening community of allies. In each community we must look within the university and act with confidence that we can be powerful, but we must look outwards to the less exotic but more lasting struggles for justice.

To turn these mythic possibilities into realities will involve national efforts at university re-form by an alliance of students and faculty. They must wrest control of the educational process from the administrative bureaucracy. They must make fraternal and functional contact with al-lies in labor, civil rights, and other liberal forces outside the campus. They must import major public issues into the curriculum—research and teaching on problems of war and peace is an outstanding example. They must make debate and controversy, not dull pedantic cant, the common style for educational life. They must consciously build a base for their assault upon the loci of power.

As students for a democratic society, we are committed to stimulating this kind of social movement, this kind of vision and program in campus and community across the country. If we appear to seek the unattainable, as it has been said, then let it be known that we do so to avoid the unimaginable.

Appendix 3

The Sharon Statement

Adopted by the Young Americans for Freedom in conference at Sharon, Conn., September 9-11, 1960

In this time of moral and political crisis, it is the responsibility of the youth of America to affirm certain eternal truths.

We, as young conservatives, believe:

That foremost among the transcendent values is the individual's use of his God-given free will, whence derives his right to be free from the restrictions of arbitrary force;

That liberty is indivisible, and that political freedom cannot long exist without economic freedom;

That the purpose of government is to protect those freedoms through the preservation of internal order, the provision of national defense, and the administration of justice;

That when government ventures beyond these rightful functions, it accumulates power, which tends to diminish order and liberty;

That the Constitution of the United States is the best arrangement yet devised for empowering government to fulfill its proper role, while restraining it from the concentration and abuse of power;

That the genius of the Constitution—the division of powers—is summed up in the clause that reserves primacy to the several states, or to the people in those spheres not specifically delegated to the Federal government;

That the market economy, allocating resources by the free play of supply and demand, is the single economic system compatible with the requirements of personal freedom and constitutional government, and that it is at the same time the most productive supplier of human needs;

That when government interferes with the work of the market economy, it tends to reduce the moral and physical strength of the nation, that when it takes from one to bestow on another, it diminishes the incentive of the first, the integrity of the second, and the moral autonomy of both;

That we will be free only so long as the national sovereignty of the United States is secure; that history shows periods of freedom are rare, and can exist only when free citizens concertedly defend their rights against all enemies;

That the forces of international Communism are, at present, the greatest single threat to these liberties;

That the United States should stress victory over, rather than coexistence with this menace; and

That American foreign policy must be judged by this criterion: does it serve the just interests of the United States?

Source: https://www.yaf.org/news/the-sharon-statement

About the Author

Richard J. Bishirjian earned a BA from the University of Pittsburgh, and a PhD in government and international studies from the University of Notre Dame where he studied with Eric Voegelin, Stanley Parry, Ralph McInerny, Henri Deku, and Gerhart Niemeyer. His PhD dissertation was completed under the direction of Gerhart Niemeyer. He did advanced study with Michael Oakeshott at the London School of Economics and studied Sanskrit at the Southern Asia Institute, Columbia University. He also studied Classical Greek at Hunter College and Latin at Loyola University of Chicago.

Dr. Bishirjian taught at universities and colleges in Indiana, Texas, and New York and is the editor of *A Public Philosophy Reader* (1978), and author of five scholarly books: *The Development of Political Theory* (1978), *The Conservative Rebellion* (2015), *The Coming Death and Future Resurrection of American Higher Education* (2017), *Ennobling Encounters* (2021), and *Rise and Fall of the American Empire* (2022). In 2020 he published *Coda*, a political novel.

Appointed to the Office of the President-Elect in 1980, Bishirjian served as a Team Leader with responsibility for the National Endowment for the Humanities and was appointed by President Reagan as acting associate director of the United States International Communication Agency, now the assistant secretary of state for Public Diplomacy. He also served on the staff of United States Senator Alfonse D'Amato (R–NY) and in the administration of President George H. W. Bush.

He served as associate director of Boston University, College of Communication, with responsibility for the College of Communication's continuing education programs in the Washington, D.C., area. In 1987, he assisted Dr. Nikolaus Lobkowicz, president of a German Catholic state university in Bavaria, to find new financing for projects in Prague and Warsaw.

In 2000, he founded Yorktown University, a for-profit internet university, raised $4 million dollars in equity financing, recruited a faculty, developed, and accredited eleven degree and certificate programs and attained national accreditation of Yorktown University. He currently serves as president of American Academy of Distance Learning.

Endnotes

[1] Michael Barone, *Our Country: The Shaping of America from Roosevelt to Reagan* (New York: The Free Press, 1990), p. 154.

[2] Anne Curry, *The Hundred Years' War* (Oxford: Osprey Publishing, 2002).

[3] Niall Ferguson, *Empire: The Rise and Demise of the British World Order and the Lessons for Global Power* (New York: Penguin Books, 2002), p. 1.

[4] Richard Bishirjian, *A Public Philosophy Reader* (New Rochelle: Arlington House, 1978).

[5] Richard Bishirjian, *The Conservative Rebellion* (South Bend: St. Augustine's Press, 2015).

[6] Daniel J. Boorstin, *The Image: A Guide to Pseudo-Events in America* (New York: Athenaeum, 1987), p. 47. Originally published in 1961 as *The Image or What Happened to the American Dream*. All page references, cited in the body of this text, are from the Athenaeum (Vintage paperback) edition.

[7] Alexis de Tocqueville, *Democracy in America*, Henry Reeve, trans. (CreateSpace Publishing, 2016). Chapter XIII: Government of the Democracy in America—Part I, p. 113.

[8] Quoted in Joseph Epstein, *Alexis De Tocqueville: Democracy's Guide* (New York: Harper Collins, 2006).

[9] Search YouTube for videos that recorded "borking" of Judge Bork: "Senate Rejects Robert Bork Nomination."

[10] Henri de Lubac, S.J. *The Drama of Atheist Humanism* (San Francisco: Ignatius Press, 1995).

[11] This discussion uses the edition of Madison's Notes edited by James McClellan and M.E. Bradford, Jonathan Elliot's *Debates in the Several State Conventions,* Vol. III, Debates in the Federal Convention of 1787 as Reported by James Madison

(Richmond, VA: James River Press, 1989). Copies of this edition priced at $40 each may be requested by email to angusmcclellan@gmail.com. Readers may want to purchase the Adrienne Koch edition of Madison's Notes published by Ohio University Press; 2nd edition (January 1, 1985). Also see James Madison's *Notes Of Debates In The Federal Convention Of 1787 And Their Relation To A More Perfect Society Of Nations*, ed. James Brown Scott (Andesite Press August 24, 2017). Ashbrook Publishing has published Gordon Lloyd's edition of Madison's Notes and has created an online directory of key documents related to the Constitutional Convention: https://teachingamericanhistory.org/wp-content/uploads/2018/08/The-Constitutional-Convention-Core-Documents.pdf. And there is an inexpensive Modern Library edition.

[12] "Framers" refers to delegates to the Philadelphia Convention of 1787. "Founding Fathers" refers to the entire generation of colonists who supported independence from the British Crown. The Congressional Research Service cites Warren Harding as the first person to refer to the "Founding Fathers."

[13] John Dos Passos, *The Head and Heart of Thomas Jefferson* (New York: Doubleday & Co., 1954), p. 306.

[14] Ibid., p. 162.

[15] Ibid., p. 336.

[16] Ibid., pp. 181–182.

[17] The reader's attention is directed to the outline of deliberations in Philadelphia found in Appendix B.

[18] David J. Siemers, *The Myth of Coequal Branches: Restoring the Constitution's Separation of Functions* (Columbia: University of Missouri Press, 2018.)

[19] Sen. Mike Lee (R-UT) who in 2016 launched something called the "Article I Project."

[20] Martin Diamond, *The Founding of the Democratic Republic* (Boston: Cengage Learning; 1 edition, January 1, 1981).

21 Cecelia M. Kenyon, ed. *The Antifederalists* (New York: Bobbs Merrill, 1966), p. 10.
22 Ibid., p. 213.
23 Ibid., p. 206.
24 Ibid., p. 206–207.
25 Ibid., p. 171.
26 Ibid., p. 18.
27 Ibid., p. 19.
28 Ibid., p. 46.
29 Ibid., p. 150.
30 Ibid., p. 154.
31 Ibid., p. 57.
32 Ibid., p. 154.
33 District ninety-six in the Constitution of South Carolina of March 26, 1776, was apportioned ten members or representatives in the General Assembly.
34 Ibid., p. 184.
35 Ibid., p. 156.
36 Ibid., p. 193.
37 Ibid., p. 187.
38 David Siemers, *The Myth of Coequal Branches: Restoring the Constitution's Separation of Functions* (Columbia: University of Missouri Press, 2018}, p. 145.
39 Ibid., p. 146.
40 Ernest Lee Tuveson, *Redeemer Nation: The Idea of America's Millennial Role* (Chicago: University of Chicago Press, 1968), p. 28, 30.
41 Tuveson, *Redeemer Nation:* pp. 53–54.
42 Robert Kagan, *Dangerous Nation* (New York: Random House, Vintage Books, 2007), p. 151. The full text of President John Quincy Adams' statement is online at http://www.presidency.ucsb.edu/ws/?pid=29467.
43 Kagan, *Dangerous Nation*, p. 169.

44 Richard M. Gamble, "Savior Nation: Woodrow Wilson and the Gospel of Service," *Humanitas* (Volume XIV, No. 1), p. 4–22.
45 Philip F. Gura, *American Transcendentalism: A History* (New York: Hill and Wang, 2007), pp. 7-8.
46 Kagan, *Dangerous Nation*, p. 256.
47 Richard Gamble, "*The Battle Hymn of the Republic* and American Civil Religion," *Modern Age*, Fall 2014 (Vol. 56, No. 4).
48 Quoted in Ernest Lee Tuveson, *Redeemer Nation. The Idea of America's Millennial Role* (Chicago: University of Chicago Press, 1968), p. 197–198.
49 *The Dial*, p. 18. All issues of *The Dial* are online at https://onlinebooks.library.upenn.edu/webbin/serial?id=thedial.
50 Kagan, *Dangerous Nation*, p. 194.
51 Richard Gamble, "Gettysburg Gospel: How Lincoln forged a civil religion of American nationalism," *The American Conservative*, November 14, 2013.
52 Kenneth R. Minoque, *Nationalism* (Baltimore, MD: Penguin Books, 1970), p. 10.
53 All citations of Wilson's speeches may be accessed from the "E-Library Search" at the website of The Woodrow Wilson Presidential Library and Museum, http://www.woodrowwilson.org/library-archives/wilson-elibrary.
54 Richard Bishirjian, "Thomas Hill Green's Political Philosophy," in *The Political Science Reviewer*, Vol. 4 (Fall 1974), pp. 29–53.
55 Mark Malvasi, "The First World War Economy & the Rise of American Power," *The Imaginative Conservative*, August 11, 2019: https://theimaginativeconservative.org/2019/08/war-economy-american-power-mark-malvasi.html.
56 Raymond Keating, *Harding, Coolidge and Economic Growth*, in "Introduction: Supply-Side from the Civil War to World War I," a course on Supply-side Economics, Yorktown University, 2012.
57 Mark Malvasi, "World War I: War as Revolution," *The Imaginative Conservative*, July 7, 2019: https://theimaginative

conservative.org/2019/07/world-war-i-woodrow-wilson-war-revolution-mark-malvasi.html.

[58] Debs was one of the founding members of the Industrial Workers of the World (IWW) and five times candidate of the Socialist Party of America for president of the United States.

[59] Mark Malvasi, "World War I: War as Revolution," *The Imaginative Conservative*, July 7, 2019: https://theimaginativeconservative.org/2019/07/world-war-i-woodrow-wilson-war-revolution-mark-malvasi.html.

[60] Richard M. Weaver, "A Dialectic on Total War," in Visions of Order: The Cultural Crisis of Our Time (Wilmington, DE, 1995; originally published in 1964), 98; qtd. In Mark Malvasi, "World War I: War as Revolution," *The Imaginative Conservative*, July 7, 2019: https://theimaginativeconservative.org/2019/07/world-war-i-woodrow-wilson-war-revolution-mark-malvasi.html.

[61] See Robert D. Cuff, "Harry Garfield, the Fuel Administration, and the Search for a Cooperative Order during World War I," American Quarterly 30 (Spring 1978), 39-53; qtd. In Mark Malvasi, "World War I: War as Revolution," *The Imaginative Conservative*, July 7, 2019: https://theimaginativeconservative.org/2019/07/world-war-i-woodrow-wilson-war-revolution-mark-malvasi.html.

[62] James Piereson, *Shattered Consensus: The Rise and Decline of America's Postwar Political Order* (New York: Encounter Books, 2015), p. 371.

[63] Ibid., 370–373.

[64] See "Scottish Philosophy in the 18th Century," *The Stanford Encyclopedia of Philosophy* online at https://plato.stanford.edu/entries/scottish-18th.

[65] Piereson, *Shattered Consensus*, p. 274.

[66] Gregory Brown, *The Progressive Era*, unpublished text for a course on Progressives at Yorktown University.

[67] Ibid., p. 275.

[68] Barone, pp. 63–68.
[69] Barone, p. 69.
[70] Ibid., p. 73.
[71] Ibid., p. 93.
[72] Ibid., p. 92.
[73] Amity Shlaes, *Great Society. A New History* (New York: HarperCollins, 2019), p. 7.
[74] Shlaes, *Great Society*, p, 319.
[75] Shlaes, *Great Society*, p, 11.
[76] Michael Harrington, *The Other America: Poverty in the United States* (New York: Penguin Specials, 1963).
[77] See Appendix.
[78] Shlaes., p. 209.
[79] Ibid., p. 295.
[80] Ibid., p. 87.
[81] Ibid., p. 89.
[82] Ibid., p. 173.
[83] Ibid., p. 283.
[84] Ibid., p. 106.
[85] Ibid., p. 107.
[86] Ibid., p. 112.
[87] M. Stanton Evans and Herbert Romerstein, *Stalin's Secret Agents: The Subversion of Roosevelt's Government* (New York: Simon and Shuster, Threshold Editions, 2012), p. 18.
[88] Ibid., p. 20.
[89] Ibid., p. 20.
[90] Ibid., p. 21.
[91] Ibid., p. 21.
[92] Ibid., p. 23.
[93] Ibid, pp. 225–229.
[94] Ibid., p. 230.
[95] Michael J. Gerson, *Heroic Conservatism*, p. 99.
[96] Ibid., p. 270.
[97] Ibid., p. 240.

[98] Ibid., p. 239.
[99] Ibid., p. 79.
[100] Walter A. McDougall, *Promised Land, Crusader State: The American Encounter with the World Since 1776* (Boston: Houghton Mifflin Harcourt, 1997), pp. 15–38. This essay is a distillation, and re-formulation, of the Introduction to my *Public Philosophy Reader* (New Rochelle, NY: Arlington House; 1st edition, 1978), a speech delivered at a regional meeting of the Philadelphia Society in Washington, DC, in 1980, subsequently published in the campus publication of Hillsdale College, *Hillsdale Review,* as well as my *History of Political Theory: A Critical Analysis* (1978).
[101] H.W. Brands, *TR. The Last Romantic* (New York: Basic Books, 1997), p. 570.
[102] Frank A. Ninkovich, *The Diplomacy of Ideas: U.S. Foreign Policy and Cultural Relations, 1938–1950* (Cambridge, Eng.: Cambridge University Press, 1981), p. 10.
[103] "United States Sovereignty and World Order," presented at the National Meeting of the Philadelphia Society 2001. Published in: Stoner, James R., Jr., *Common Law and Liberal Theory: Coke, Hobbes, and the Origins of American Constitutionalism* (Lawrence, Kan., 1992).
[104] Norman A. Graebner, ed., *Ideas and Diplomacy: Readings in the Intellectual Tradition of American Foreign Policy* (New York, 1964), pp. 406–417.
[105] Michael D. Tanner, "At Last a Small-Government Conservative?" Cato Institute. (September 12, 2007.) https://www.cato.org/commentary/last-small-government-conservative
[106] Online at www.fas.org/irp/world/para/docs/980223-fatwa.htm
[107] Online at www.meforum.org/article/646
[108] Originally published as *Wissenschaft, Politik and Gnosis* (Munich: Kosel-Verlag, 1959), English edition, William J.

Fitzpatrick, trans. *Science, Politics and Gnosticism. Two Essays.* Chicago: Henry Refinery Co., Gateway Edition, 1968).

[109] Plato, *The Republic,* 529c.

[110] Richard J. Bishirjian, *Modern Age,* Spring 2019, pp. 36-41. https://isi.org/modern-age/prelude-to-civil-war-francis-graham-wilson-on-spain/.

[111] Irving Kristol, *On the Democratic Idea in America* (New York: Harper & Row, 1972), p. 51.

[112] Aristotle, *Nicomachean Ethics,* 1134b16–1135a5.

[113] Thomas K. McGraw, "The Progressive Legacy," Lewis L. Gould, ed., *The Progressive Era* (Syracuse, NY: Syracuse University Press, 1974).

[114] See Ralph Rossum, "The Seventeenth Amendment and the Death of Freedom," prepared for delivery at the Panel on "Republicanism, Federalism, and the Constitution" at the 2003 Fall Regional Meeting of the Philadelphia Society: https://phillysoc.org/voices-of-conservatism/?speaker_id=4377 And see Ralph A. Rossum, *Federalism, the Supreme Court and the Seventeenth Amendment: The Irony of Constitutional Democracy* (Lanham, MD: Lexington Books, 2001).

www.ingramcontent.com/pod-product-compliance
Lightning Source LLC
Chambersburg PA
CBHW071200160426
43196CB00011B/2144